Finding Forgiveness

To Jenni,

Every Blessing,

Jim macdonald

Other titles in this series, available from
Redemptorist Publications:

The Inside Job: A Spirituality of True Self-Esteem

(Available Autumn 2007)
Achieving Life's Purpose: Spirituality in Later Life

Finding Forgiveness:
Personal and Spiritual Perspectives

Jim McManus
&
Stephanie Thornton

A Redemptorist Publication

Published by **Redemptorist Publications**

Copyright © 2006 Redemptorist Publications

Cover design: Arcus Design
Design: Peena Lad

ISBN 0 85231 315 2

Printed by Cambridge University Press

Redemptorist
PUBLICATIONS

Alphonsus House Chawton Hampshire GU34 3HQ
Telephone 01420 88222   Fax 01420 88805
rp@rpbooks.co.uk   www.rpbooks.co.uk

We dedicate this book to those who have shared their journey to forgiveness with us and also to those who have helped us in the preparation of this book, especially to Michael, Simon and Myles.

Contents

		Page
Preface		11
1	**The invitation to forgiveness**	13
	The gift of forgiveness	13
	What has forgiveness to do with spiritual fulfilment?	15
	Jesus' offering of forgiveness	16
	The transforming power of forgiveness	18
	Finding forgiveness	20
	Exercise	21
2	**Forgiveness and revenge**	24
	The problem of forgiveness	26
	Overreacting	28
	An eye for an eye and a tooth for a tooth	30
	Breaking the cycle	32
	Christ and forgiveness	33
	Our right to forgiveness	35
	Exercise	36
3	**The shape of forgiveness**	38
	Wisdom of the ages	39
	Hinduism	39
	Buddhism	40
	The Abrahamic religions	42
	1. Judaism	42
	2. Islam	43
	3. Christianity	43
	The route to spirituality	44
	The nature of forgiveness	47
	Forgiveness is not... forgetting	47
	Forgiveness is... about coming to terms with reality	47

Forgiveness does not…
let the offender "off the hook"   48
Forgiveness… sets the victim free   49
Forgiveness is not… reconciliation   50
Forgiveness is… strength   50
Forgiveness… cannot be a moral duty
imposed upon us   51
Forgiveness… stems from the decision
to forgive   51
Living examples   52
Exercise   54

4   Science and forgiveness   55
Letting go of negativity: why me?   56
Why should I forgive, when I am
the victim?   56
Forgiveness heals   57
Forgiveness and the body   58
Forgiveness and mental health   59
Forgiveness and society   60
Forgiveness and being forgiven   60
Psychology and forgiveness   61
Personality and forgiveness   62
Forgiveness and maturity   64
Empathy and forgiveness   66
Is forgiveness always healing?   67
Letting go of grievance:
forgiveness and forgetting   68
Forgiving and reconciling   70
Forgiveness and repentance   71
Science, spirituality and forgiveness   72
Exercise   72

5 The process of forgiveness   75

Accepting different paths to forgiveness   75
    Living forgiveness   75
    Shocked into forgiveness   76
    Struggling to forgive   78
The natural process of forgiveness   80
    Stage one – Denial   80
    Stage two – Self-blame   82
    Stage three – Victimhood   83
    Stage four – Indignation   85
    Stage five – Surviving   86
    Stage six – Reintegration   88
    Stage seven – Forgiveness   91
How to speed the process of forgiveness?   91
    Harnessing the natural processes
    of forgiveness   92
    Harnessing spiritual resources
    for forgiveness   93
Exercise   95

6 Accepting the gift of forgiveness   97

Facing the need for forgiveness   97
    The pain of unforgiveness   99
Finding comfort through forgiveness   99
    Inner healing   100
Ongoing change: conversion   102
    Doing it over and over again   102
    Conversion and change   103
Opening the door to spirituality   105
Exercise   106

**7 The grace to forgive: a Catholic
perspective**   107

Grace builds on nature   107
Individualistic notions of salvation   108
Definition of the Church   108

Priority of God's forgiveness 109
Forgiving the unrepentant 110
    A Christian Armenian witness 112
The sacramental dimension of Christian
forgiveness 112
    The first sacrament of forgiveness 113
Christ acting in us 114
    The role of the Holy Spirit in our lives 115
    The Holy Spirit is the New Covenant 116
Grace and forgiveness 117
    Sacrament of confirmation 119
    Confirmation as the completion of
    baptism 120
    Sacrament of reconciliation 122
Healing the wound of sin 125
    New emphasis in the sacrament
    of reconciliation 125
    The Holy Eucharist 128
    The presence of God 129
    Forgiveness presumed as we share
    in the Eucharist 131
    Deeper union with Christ 132
A Christian witness from San Salvador 133
Exercise 134

8 Finding forgiveness in prayer 136
How to praise God 136
Teaching of St Patrick 137
The God who forgives 138
The God who heals 139
A consoling image 141
Healing our image of God 142
How God deals with our sins 144
Exercise 146

About the Authors 148

Preface

Our aim in writing this book on forgiveness is pastoral. That is, we want this book to be helpful to those who need to engage again with forgiveness in their lives, and at the same time we want it to help those who are seeking to help others to approach the possibility of forgiveness in their lives.

There have probably been times in all our lives when we were personally challenged in the area of forgiveness. We may have known people living morally impeccable lives, with deep religious conviction and spirituality, who, when confronted with the challenge of forgiving, have been unable to do so – with disastrous consequences: families traumatised; lifelong friendships broken; long-term relationships in acrimony. People who have been well trained to cope with life's unexpected twists and turns, either professionally, through their education, or religiously, through their church's teaching, often display a truly puzzling inability to cope with the challenge of forgiveness.

There are good Christian people who have had to refrain from saying the Lord's Prayer because they could not bring themselves to say "forgive us our trespasses, as we forgive those who trespass against us". Also, there are those who refuse to offer the sign of peace during Mass to someone who has hurt or upset them. While such good people would never seek to reconcile a life of stealing with their moral or religious convictions, they seem, in some extraordinary way, able to reconcile a life of unforgiveness with their moral and religious outlook.

So often a hurt person's refusal even to consider forgiveness stems from the pain of the hurt. Their trust and confidence in someone they loved have been shattered and the only way they know how to get on with life is to lock themselves into unforgiveness. They are suffering from a broken heart rather than a hard heart. At other times, even theologically educated people have a glaring misunderstanding of the nature and process of forgiveness. They secretly feel that by forgiving a wrong in some way, they are condoning it or minimising it or letting the guilty party "off the hook".

The authors are also aware that, although forgiveness is at the heart of the gospel of Jesus Christ, church ministers of all denominations have become strangely reticent about it. If we were to ask churchgoers, "When did you last hear a full sermon on forgiveness, on the need for you to forgive the person who offended you?" we would most likely get the answer, "I can never remember hearing such a sermon." We believe that this great pulpit silence on forgiveness is really due to the hundred-year silence of psychology on this fundamental human activity. Since psychologists were ignoring it, and even dismissing it, psychologically literate pastors began to be weary of it. They began to feel that the message of forgiveness would not be Good News for the badly hurt person. To borrow John Cleese's way with words in *Fawlty Towers,* "Whatever you do, don't mention ... forgiveness!"

Now that psychology is beginning to explore the healing power of forgiveness, church ministers, both ordained and lay, have a golden opportunity to preach and teach the gospel message with renewed conviction. Our hope is that our explorations of the nature and the process of forgiveness will encourage and help them to do this.

We wish to express our gratitude to the many men and women, some of whom are mentioned in our text, who have shared their forgiveness struggle with us. We have learned a great deal about the nature and process of forgiveness by being privileged to listen to the pain in their hearts and to witness the liberation that forgiveness brought. They were our best teachers.

We are also grateful to Marguerite Hutchinson, the Commissioning Editor at Redemptorist Publications, for her encouragement in writing this book, and to Caroline Hodgson, who took her place when she went on maternity leave.

1

The invitation to forgiveness

"... to live, to love, is to be failed, to forgive, to have failed,
to be forgiven, for ever and ever ..."
Gillian Rose, 1997, *Love's Work*

Our human experience is so very often one of being let down by other
people: of being betrayed in our hopes of love, our expectations of
respect or consideration, in extreme cases deprived of our livelihood or
even of health or life itself. Equally, our experience is of having failed
in some way, having let others down or behaved badly. Which of us
cannot think of wrongs done to us, injustices large or small that we
have suffered? Which of us cannot bring to mind things we regret doing
– or failing to do – that caused suffering?

So much pain comes into human lives from this feeling of having been
failed, or failing! What if it weren't like that? What would your life be
like, if you carried no resentment towards yourself or anyone else,
harboured no grievances? What if you could truly forgive not only all
the injuries and insults you have suffered, but also all the failures and
inadequacies you see in yourself?

The gift of forgiveness

Sometimes when we are in pain forgiveness is the last thing we think
of, the last thing we feel capable of offering. Why *should* I forgive,
when I have been so unjustly wounded, so deeply hurt? How *can* I
forgive, when those who have so unjustly harmed me go about life
unrepentant, unpunished? How can I – or anyone else – forgive *me* for
what I have done, or what I have failed to do?

Such feelings are natural, but they rest on a misunderstanding of what forgiveness is, and of what it does for us. Forgiveness is not a burden, not a difficult sacrifice that lets the transgressor off the hook. Rather it is a healing gift for the one who forgives: it is the forgiver who is set free from pain. It is I who am healed when I forgive those who have wounded me or let me down. It is I who am healed when I forgive myself for causing wounds or letting myself down. Without the healing gift of forgiveness I am trapped in pain and grievance against others, or against myself – a profound alienation. Letting go of this pain sets me free to grow healthily again.

Moreover, the gift of forgiveness has a dimension that extends far, far beyond psychological healing, important as that human healing is. Forgiveness is the gift of God, a gift freely extended to us and flowing through us to others. In forgiving we accord others a value and respect that transcend their particular actions or characteristics. In being forgiven, the truth that we ourselves have a value that transcends our actions is endorsed. In accepting the forgiveness of God, the nature of our true selves is revealed, transcending human limitations.

Through this book we invite you to explore with us the true nature of forgiveness. Together we will explore the paths leading to forgiveness, and the attainment of its fullest fruits. The authors of this book are Christians and, specifically, Catholics. For us, forgiveness is at the heart of spirituality, at the heart of our relationship with God and with one another. You are free to share or reject our beliefs! But we hope that you will come to understand them, and to understand the power of Christ's message.

We believe that forgiveness is at the very centre of what makes a good human life. It's the salve that heals our wounds. More than this: we believe that the giving and receiving of forgiveness is at the heart of spirituality, the gateway to spiritual fulfilment, to union with God. Becoming a forgiving person – a person who forgives others, a person who forgives oneself, a person who embraces the forgiveness of God – is the key.

What has forgiveness to do with spiritual fulfilment?

For many people, the idea that forgiveness is at the heart of a healthy spirituality comes as a surprise. Why so? How so? The answer has already been given: we all have a value that transcends our human limitations.

We are biological beings, possessed of bodies that wax and wane, grow strong and beautiful, rot and decay. We are also psychological beings, possessed of characteristics, capable of actions that may be glorious or shameful, heroic or despicable, useful or pointless. Above all, we are spiritual beings, possessed of characteristics that transcend our bodies, transcend the events and actions of our lives. This last is a truth that many find hard to accept; and that lack of acceptance is a key barrier to forgiveness – of others, or ourselves.

If we were to suggest that you are no more than your physical body, that your value and worth are defined by that body, you would be (rightly) outraged. To treat another person as no more than a beautiful or sexually attractive object; no more than a strong back to slave in factory or field; no more than a creature reduced by old age, illness or injury – such things appal all but the most shallow among us. No! We are creatures with personalities, feelings, needs, fears, gifts and talents that transcend our bodily limitations! *You cannot judge a book by its cover*. Rich treasure and value may be hidden in all of us, however we look.

The idea that our psychological characteristics and hence our human value cannot be assessed from our bodily state is now almost universally accepted, though this was not always so! But we are less open to the idea that our psychological characteristics may be as irrelevant to our ultimate value   which is to say our spiritual value – as our bodily state is to our psychological value. Surely, if a person behaves badly he or she is *bad*?

If we were to suggest that you are no more than one particular action, no more than one particular mistake or transgression, no more than one flawed psychological characteristic, you would (rightly) protest: *I am so much more than that!* However badly a person behaves, the bad behaviour does not wholly define him or her. Even the most evil man or woman may sometimes show kindness. Inherent in all of us is the capacity for good and bad behaviour to some degree. No past action or characteristic defines who or what we are, any more than our present physical body defines our scope. We are, all of us, more than our actions, more than our psychological characteristics. We have inherent potential, and hence a value that transcends those specific things.

For Christians, that inherent potential and value is a reflection of our true selves – the selves that transcend particular events or circumstances, transcend our particular actions and characteristics. Our inherent potential, our ultimate value, stems from the nature of our being. We are made in the image of God, with the capacity, to grow in that image. It is this stunning inheritance, this stunning capacity, that underwrites our ultimate spiritual value. In recognising this inherent potential, this ultimate value in ourselves and others, we begin to engage with life on a powerfully spiritual level. And it is through *forgiveness* that we transcend the particulars of psychological actions and characteristics (ours, or other people's) to catch a glimpse of our spiritual legacy, to see ourselves in God's eyes – for we are precious in God's eyes.

Jesus' offering of forgiveness

Unconditional forgiveness reflecting our value in God's eyes is at the very heart of Christ's teaching. It is the core of Christianity. Jesus never asks, "What have you done?" He just offers absolute and unconditional forgiveness and invites us to come back to God:

> Just then some men came, carrying a paralysed man on a bed. They were trying to bring him in and lay him before Jesus; but

finding no way to bring him in because of the crowd, they went up on the roof and let him down with his bed through the tiles into the middle of the crowd in front of Jesus. When he saw their faith, he said, "Friend, your sins are forgiven you." Then the scribes and the Pharisees began to question, "Who is this who is speaking blasphemies? Who can forgive sins but God alone?" When Jesus perceived their questionings, he answered them, "Why do you raise such questions in your hearts? Which is easier, to say, 'Your sins are forgiven you,' or to say, 'Stand up and walk'? But so that you may know that the Son of Man has authority on earth to forgive sins" – he said to the one who was paralysed – "I say to you, stand up and take your bed and go to your home." Immediately he stood up before them, took what he had been lying on, and went to his home, glorifying God. (Luke 5:18-25)

Who knows how this man became paralysed, or what burden of guilt he was carrying? For Jesus, the one was as irrelevant as the other. Christ simply offers healing and forgiveness. And that is what he offers to each one of us: absolute, unconditional forgiveness – if we will reach out for it, if we can accept what is offered.

As Christians, we believe that, whatever we may feel, we are *always* at home in God's loving embrace: endlessly and unconditionally enfolded in God's love and forgiveness. But to experience that love and forgiveness, and the great peace and joy that they bring, our hearts must be open and receptive. To be *receptive* to love and forgiveness, our hearts must be open to the presence within us of God's Spirit. A heart focused on hate and unforgiveness will find only hate and unforgiveness – just as a person focused on stones will find only stones and miss the flowers growing among them. Only a heart oriented to love and forgiveness is open to finding those blessings.

This is why Jesus urges us to be forgiving, and to forgive as endlessly and unconditionally as we are ourselves forgiven – to forgive "not seven times, but, I tell you, seventy-seven times" (Matthew 18:22).

It is why, in the prayer Jesus taught us, we pray: "Forgive us our trespasses as we forgive those who trespass against us." It is why Jesus tells us to keep our hearts open to receive forgiveness, to recognise our need for that divine and absolute forgiveness that surpasses anything we could ever deserve, as in the constant prayer of the Church: Lord, have mercy; Christ, have mercy.

Although, as the quote from Gillian Rose at the beginning of this chapter shows, the implied emphasis on our failures – the sins that alienate us from God – can seem negative at first, the message of this prayer is anything but negative: forgiveness is not penance, and recognising the need to be forgiven is not self-abasement, not a devaluing of self. Quite the reverse! Opening our hearts to offer and receive forgiveness clears the way for us to receive a blessing beyond imagination. It is the key to bringing fullness of meaning and value to life, to feeling ourselves transformed by God's healing, forgiving love, transcending our physical and psychological limitations and restoring us to our true selves.

The transforming power of forgiveness

The power of forgiveness to heal, to connect us more directly to our spiritual values, is wonderfully illustrated by the life of Michael McGoldrick, a Catholic whose son was murdered in Northern Ireland. Michael tells his story:

> We turned on our TV and heard that a taxi driver had been murdered. I didn't think it could be anyone who belonged to us or we would have heard. But the news report continued, "Taxi driver, married with one child, wife expecting another baby ..." My wife Bridie and I just looked at each other in cold denial. Then the next sentence came, "He had just graduated from university on Friday." It was our son. I looked at my wife and said, "We'll never smile again." The next day Bridie and I made the decision to take our own lives, because Michael was everything we had. Bridie

suffers from arthritis and had plenty of tablets. But as I went out to the kitchen, suddenly a picture of the crucified Christ came into my mind. It hit me that God's Son, too, had been murdered – for us. I knew that what we planned to do was wrong. It still amazes me how God intervened in such a miraculous way to change our minds. Before they closed my son's coffin, I laid my hands on his and said, "Goodbye son, I'll see you in heaven." At that very moment I experienced the power of God coursing through my body. I was filled with a great sense of joy and confidence in God. I felt as if I could have faced Goliath – I never felt so strong in my whole life. On the morning of the funeral, I wrote on the back of an envelope a word which came to me so calm and clear, referring to those who had murdered Michael: "Bury your pride with my son." At the bottom I wrote: "Forgive them." I felt that, despite the agony we were going through, God had given me a message of peace, forgiveness and reconciliation. I spoke that message in front of the TV cameras that morning, and I still stand by it. Every morning I ask God to continue to give me the grace to forgive those who murdered my child. The power and grace I experienced to forgive from the heart was such a freedom and release. I know that resentment and bitterness would have killed me. After my son's murder, God gave me a clear grasp of the horror of sin, and I remember saying to God: "These hands will never do any evil again." I realised that in the same way I had offered forgiveness to those who killed my son, God had forgiven me my sin. Sometimes it's impossible for us to carry alone the burden of grief thrust upon us. We have to give it up and I have discovered that the best person to give it to is God. He completely takes if off your shoulders and points you in a different direction. Since Michael's death, I have been a changed man. Along with Bridie I started a relief ministry to orphanages in Romania. I feel as if Christ has taken hold of my life and I now want to take hold of Christ and give my life to loving God and serving people.[1]

Michael is a witness to the healing power of forgiveness: his life took on a new meaning, his heart was freed from bitterness, he began to feel compassion for orphans in Romania rather than wallow in self-pity, he began a new life rather than end his existing life, as he was sorely tempted to do – that was a great victory of grace. He identifies the first beneficiary of forgiving: "I know that resentment and bitterness would have killed me." Michael and Bridie were healed through the power of forgiving love, and even though those who murdered their son had no remorse and will never say sorry, their forgiveness was unconditional. They realised that they had an inalienable right to forgive and by exercising their right they brought healing and wholeness to their lives.

Unforgiveness would have been an insurmountable barrier to their healing. Nobody could forgive for them. Only they could take responsibility for forgiving or for refusing to forgive. Michael sees his and Bridie's forgiveness as a direct intervention of God: "It amazes me how God intervened in such a miraculous way to change our minds." Had Michael not forgiven he would have been crippled by resentments and bitterness. And sadly, many people would have supported him in refusing to forgive. Many people believe that it is impossible to forgive such a horrendous act as the murder of one's child. But Michael and Bridie give shining witness to the power of grace, and indeed, to the power of our own innate goodness, once it is open to grace.

Many people, seeking inner healing, want the pain and the bitterness to be taken away, even exorcised, without their having to take responsibility for their lives, and without allowing forgiveness to give them a whole new direction in life. It is very easy for them to attribute their inner pain to an evil spirit or external events and not to their own refusal to forgive.

Finding forgiveness
As we shall see throughout this book, there are many stories of the healing power of forgiveness that are as remarkable, and as

transforming, as Michael McGoldrick's. But for many of us, the possibility of forgiving anything so terrible – or even of forgiving much lesser things – seems unimaginable. How often do we say, or feel in our hearts: *that's unforgivable!* How hard it seems to move forward beyond that point and travel towards the forgiveness and joy that Michael expresses.

This book is about that journey into forgiveness. For some, forgiveness comes as a sudden grace from God, as it did for Michael. For many, finding forgiveness is a longer journey: effortful and slow, a challenge to be met. Sudden or slow, no one can make the journey of forgiveness for us. We must each find the courage and faith to open our hearts to receive that healing grace. But we need not search for those things alone. Together, we shall explore our need to give and to receive forgiveness, our need to open our hearts to the grace of forgiveness. We shall explore the conundrums forgiveness presents to us: is it always right, or even possible, to forgive? Aren't there, really, some things that are beyond forgiveness? We shall explore what forgiveness demands, what it is, and, equally importantly, what it is not. We shall look at how forgiveness has been understood in different times and traditions. We shall explore what happens in our human hearts and minds as we strive towards forgiveness. We shall explore what it means to find true forgiveness in God.

EXERCISE

Let us begin by centring ourselves: learning to create a space ready for the work of forgiveness:

- Choose a time when you have ten minutes or so to spare. Find a quiet place, somewhere as free of interruptions and disruptions as possible. Sit in a comfortable chair, with your spine upright, your two feet firmly on the floor, your arms relaxed by your side. Close your eyes.

- Feel the tension in your feet and ankles. Let that tension go: let your muscles relax, and feel the tension flow out from your feet and ankles to the earth. Now focus on your legs and do the same thing: feel the tension in the muscles, and let it go; relax and let the tension flow out through your legs to the earth. Now do the same thing with your hips, and then your spine, your chest, your arms and hands, your neck. Feel the tension around your jaw, your eyes; let it go, relax, let it flow away through your body and into the earth.

- Notice your breathing. Don't try to change it. Just listen to the rhythms of your body as you relax.

- Notice the sounds that come from outside, and from inside the room. And now go back to paying attention to your breathing.

- Sit quietly like this for a while. What is passing through your mind? Maybe there is nothing there except a stillness. Or maybe you have some thought or image, or some feeling or emotion. Notice what it is and accept it.

- Bring your thoughts back to your breathing and relax.

- And then gradually return to the world.

This technique for deep relaxation may be familiar to you. It is a practice common to many religions, and many non-religious approaches to spiritual questions. It should leave you very calm, and very aware of yourself at many different levels: body, mind, spirit. This is an excellent place from which to start our work towards a stronger spirituality through forgiveness. It is also one of the oldest forms of prayer: the oldest form of Christian prayer. Let us call it our "centring" prayer.

Note

1   Michael McGoldrick, "Grace to forgive – Strength to go on", *Power to Change Website* [online Christian resource] (n.d.) <http://www.powertochange.ie/changed/michael_mcgoldrick.html>, accessed 25 Oct. 2005.

2

Forgiveness and revenge

"God wasn't a Christian, then."
A small child, responding to biblical descriptions of "eye for an eye"
responses to insult and injury in the Old Testament

Talk about forgiveness has become fashionable in recent history. We've had, and admired, the reconciliation tribunals in South Africa where individuals confessed their actions and were forgiven, or at least granted amnesty, and re-embraced into society. We've experienced a pope, John Paul II, personally forgiving the man who shot him and apologising and seeking forgiveness for mistaken actions of the Catholic Church going back to the Crusades. And then there is the forgiveness project, which lists so many heart-warming examples from all around the world of people forgiving what seems unforgivable. Whether we achieve it or not, our generation is highly aware of the merits of striving for forgiveness.[1]

It wasn't always so. The very idea of forgiving those who offend us has often been seen as quite outrageous, even wrong-headed. Surely we have a right to hold a grievance against those who do wrong by us? Surely we have a right to that anger, and to some form of retribution or revenge? Such difference of opinion about the very idea of forgiveness comes through clearly in memories of a sabbatical course in 1987 at the University of California, Berkeley:

> I was attending a course with an interesting title: "The dialogue between Theology and Psychology". I was the only Catholic priest on the course. There were two Catholic sisters and the other thirteen members of the class were ministers in their various Churches. The lecturer, a professor, was a priest in her own Church and she was a therapist on the campus. As well as giving

some theory, she also shared with us some of her case work, demonstrating how she counselled men and women in different traumatic situations. One case concerned a woman who had suffered egregious sexual abuse from her own father for several years while she was growing up. As a little girl she repressed that entire trauma and went on to have a successful career. But her childhood was coming back to undermine her: she came to our professor for therapy.

The professor was explaining the various stages of therapy that she was taking her client through. I was waiting to see if there would be any connections with the inner healing process, with which I was familiar, but none was appearing. One day she said that they had now completed all the stages and that they would just meet once again for a little ritual of separation. I realised that I had to ask my question then. When I asked her at what stage would she speak to her client about forgiveness she became very angry and banged the table exclaiming, "I don't go in for cheap forgiveness!" Her reaction took me aback, but it also raised my temper. So, I shouted back, "I didn't say 'cheap forgiveness', I said 'forgiveness', and it wasn't cheap, because it came through the cross of Jesus Christ." By this stage every single person in the class was round my head like a swarm of hornets round a nest. I had used the "F" word! Up until that moment I had no idea that forgiveness was held in such suspicion and ridicule. At one stage the lecturer said, "She has nothing to forgive. Her father does not exist!" Still smarting under the attack I said, "I joined this class because of the title, and Jesus Christ hasn't got a word in all term. Why do you call it theology?" As we all began to simmer down the lecturer said, "Jim obviously feels very strongly about this, so, let us give our session next week to forgiveness." When we came back the following week we had a reasonable discussion on forgiveness. Then, at the end of the term, and this is the point of this story, she invited us all along to her rooms for a celebration.

As she was thanking us all for taking part in her course she said to me, "I can guarantee you that this is the only institute in the whole of the USA that will have given one hour to forgiveness this year." At that moment I realised that we had a long road to travel if we wished to retrieve forgiveness for God's wounded people.[2]

This story illustrates the fact that even highly intelligent, well-meaning people trained as healers and even followers of Christ don't always accept the need for forgiveness, the need to let go of grievances and move on. Why so?

The problem of forgiveness
What do we do, when someone attacks us, wounds us? How do we respond?

A toddler at play snatches a toy from another child. Outraged, the child snatches it back – and soon the two are pushing, screaming, shoving, hitting, biting … childish behaviour! But so many adults, too, can behave just like this, can even enshrine this tit for tat in social mores or even in laws.

The trouble with being attacked is that, as with these toddlers, it upsets us. Very often, it triggers feelings of outrage and hurt, unleashing anger that demands retribution. Like the toddlers, we begin by trying to right the wrong, and slip easily into vengeful punishment of the wrongdoer – punishment that offends the original transgressor, in turn, so that the situation escalates out of control. Forgiveness does not come easily to mind in the heat of such moments!

This emotional response to being attacked is almost instinctive in us. Take my toy, and in my anger I will grab it back. Resist, and I will punish your outrageous behaviour with a blow. This basic formula is the root of the age-old tradition of vendetta or blood feud in the adult world: harm me, and I feel that I have the right to harm you right back, in exactly the same way. Harm my kin, and I assume the right to harm yours in return; I may even feel *obligated* to make you and your kin pay in kind for the harm you have done to me and mine. What is so very wrong with this? Surely it's only natural to be enraged by other people's bad behaviour, to strike back? Let's leave our values aside for a moment. From a purely practical point of view, the trouble is that this type of tit-for-tat response elicits more of the same. And that will be just as true whether we were the victims of the original attack, or whether we were attacked in revenge for our own bad behaviour. This kind of revenge can create an endless cycle of attack and counter-attack, escalating out of all proportion to the initial incident. We'd do well always to remember the wise saying of the Chinese philosopher Confucius: "If you devote your life to seeking revenge, first dig two graves." This is the territory of vendetta, blood feud.

Vendettas, blood feuds, the remorseless pursuit of revenge have all been a persistent blight throughout human history, and they create a cycle of hatred and destruction that can persist for years – even for centuries – generation after generation, long after the original injury has been forgotten. It's easiest to see this when it happens on a large scale: where a whole community pursues a vendetta against another community (as in Rwanda, the former Yugoslavia, and many other places). But on a smaller scale, such things happen within families or between neighbours or colleagues and they blight lives.

Of course, *something* must be done when we are attacked out of the blue. If we simply ignore the offence, we leave the wrongdoer free to offend again, and we leave ourselves very exposed and vulnerable. The right to defend ourselves is universally recognised. As Pope John Paul II put it: "Legitimate self-defence can be not only a right but a duty for someone responsible for another's life, the common good of the family or the state."[3] But what is "legitimate self-defence"? How far can we go to defend ourselves? How can we control our outrage, our vengeance, limit ourselves to a reasonable response, a legitimate self-defence?

These issues are at the core of the problem with forgiveness. Often we don't know what is, or is not, a legitimate response of self-defence.

Often, too, we can't control our emotions and respond from rage rather than reason. Our rage seems reasonable and justified to us, as do the actions that that rage drives – however destructive they may be. And because our rage seems reasonable and justified, letting go of our grievances and *forgiving* is often very far off the agenda.

Overreacting

The destructive cycle of revenge is bad enough when it is a reaction in proportion to the wound we have suffered – a toy snatched back from the thief, a shove for a shove. But rage so often takes us beyond responding proportionately. Enraged, we may be driven only to harm the other – easily slipping towards inflicting wounds that far exceed the injuries we have ourselves received. History is rich in examples of such overreactions, from the murder of whole villages – men, women and children – in retribution for the assassination of one soldier in Hitler's Europe, to the "execution" of thousands of innocents by politically motivated terrorists.

Nor is the problem new: here are the words of that strange character Lamech, from the very first book of the Bible, Genesis:

> Adah and Zillah, hear my voice;
> you wives of Lamech, listen to what I say:
> I have killed a man for wounding me,
> a young man for striking me.
> If Cain is avenged sevenfold,
> truly Lamech seventy-sevenfold. (Genesis 4:23-24)

In our everyday lives, too, we can often overreact. Sometimes the overreaction is obvious: "A while back, my son, then a new driver, forgot to signal a right turn on a roundabout and mildly inconvenienced another driver as a result. That other driver pursued him in his car, hooting his horn and gesticulating aggressively. Eventually, at a traffic light, the pursuing driver jumped out of his car and tried to hit my son."[4] Such over-the-top episodes of "road rage" are sadly becoming more common. People have even been stabbed or killed because they were careless in their driving, or forgot to signal.

Often, we simply don't notice that our response to a hurt is an overreaction. Someone says or does something that hurts or offends us, and we let a sense of grievance take root in our heart, creating a wound that is out of all proportion to the event that inflicted it, a wound that feeds an angry vengeance as disproportionate as that road-rage driver's. It's hard to detect such moments in one's own life. After all, *my* overreaction usually seems entirely reasonable to *me*, at least at the time! A man – let's call him Fred – remembers just such an incident:

> I was helping a friend to wallpaper her new house. I was struggling a bit to reach the top of the wall on the landing, and things were going much more slowly than I'd hoped. Suddenly I heard her on the phone inviting other friends over, saying she could do with more help. I was furious! I assumed that she thought I couldn't manage, that she was criticising me. I really saw red, and attacked her fiercely for her rudeness and lack of confidence in me. She was stunned and confused – I didn't explain why I was so angry, it seemed so obvious. The fact that she said she couldn't understand why I was upset seemed deceitful to me, so I just got angrier and angrier and was more and more spiteful. The rest of the morning was awful, the atmosphere terrible, and I was very rude to the other people when they arrived. Then I realised that I had got the whole situation wrong: she hadn't asked them to take over or even help with the wallpapering and hadn't criticised my efforts there at all! The other friends had offered to help unpack and wash china – nothing to do with me. I had misunderstood and taken hurt where none was intended, and given back spite and anger. And looking back, I can see that, even if she had looked for someone to help me, my reaction would have been over the top: irritation surely doesn't justify such widespread spite. In fact, of course, I could have seen the whole situation very

differently. I could have seen having a helper as a bonus rather than a criticism: it was a difficult job, easier for two. It was my own pride that hurt me, and my own anger that created pain. We've got over the incident, but the friendships aren't the same now. It's hard for me to forget such a horrible misunderstanding, what a fool I made of myself. And it's hard for the others to forget how spiteful I was.[5]

Fred admits that he is a touchy man, easily convinced that other people are finding fault with him. But most of us have, to some degree, the same tendency to see things only from our own perspective, ready to notice hurts and attacks, and to react with resentment, punishing the "crime" disproportionately. Most of us can probably think of episodes in our own lives where we have overreacted to a real hurt, or perceived hurt where none was intended. Most of us, like Fred, could identify a real price we have paid for this.

An eye for an eye and a tooth for a tooth

We mistakenly tend to think of the Old Testament saying "An eye for an eye and a tooth for a tooth" (as quoted by Jesus in Matthew 5:38) as somehow justifying our feeling that we are entitled to hate, and to strike back when someone injures us. But in fact, this principle was intended to *limit* acts of revenge – to prevent overreactions. It was never meant to be taken literally. Shylock's "pound of flesh" in Shakespeare's *Merchant of Venice* had no justification in Old Testament morality. Regrettably the maxim "an eye for an eye", or the *lex talionis*, as it was called, was used in anti-Jewish propaganda throughout history. While the Old Testament acknowledges the anger and hurt of the victim and allows for a *proportional* response, it repudiates the blood feud or the vendetta.

In many ways, limiting revenge to what is proportionate to the original crime is a very good thing. In the story of the young driver described earlier, a mere "eye for an eye", a mere forgotten traffic signal for a forgotten traffic signal, would have looked reasonable and moderate! There's a lot to be said for limiting vengeance and anger to a proportional response, taking (figuratively) *only* "an eye for an eye", giving only a small hurt where a small hurt was received, reacting only when there has been a real attack, rather than an imagined one.

But even this "equitable" level of retaliation is costly! In everyday matters, no one dies, nor, usually, suffers much material harm. But what is the effect on our quality of life, our feelings of value? What is the spiritual cost of even "reasonable" retaliation? Do we feel *better*, after striking a friend off our Christmas list, or hurling abuse at another driver, or criticising a friend? How could behaviour which would appal us in someone else be acceptable in ourselves?

We make excuses for our own bad behaviour that we would not allow for other people: we attribute their faults to their personalities, and our own faults to circumstances. If *you* indulge in road rage, gesturing aggressively at me, I see you as an unattractive, aggressive person. If *I* do exactly the same thing, I see that as the result of all the stress I'm under. Nonetheless, for most of us there is a residue of pain, regret, even shame after such episodes of bad behaviour. And very often, our retaliation – even when it is in response to a real attack, and in proportion to that attack – sets up a pattern: our grievance and revenge hurt others, a new hurt that feeds and recycles back through them to hurt us again, fuelling endless pain. Through feeding rage this way, we separate ourselves from those feelings of love and respect that are at the heart of healthy spirituality.

The poet Seamus Heaney captured the yearning to live beyond vengeance with this poem:

> History says, don't hope
> On this side of the grave.
> But then, once in a lifetime
> The longed-for tidal wave
> Of justice can rise up.

And hope and history rhyme,
So hope for a great sea-change
On the far side of revenge.
Believe that a further shore
Is reachable from here.[6]

Breaking the cycle

There is only one way out of this negative spiral, and that is to refuse to play that game. In other words, to refuse to live by the law of retaliation, to refuse to give back blow for blow, to refuse to devalue others because they have behaved badly, to refuse to devalue ourselves by behaving badly in return. This is what we mean by forgiveness. And this is why all the major religions of the world hold a special place for forgiveness in their teachings.

As the Jewish philosopher Hannah Arendt said, "Forgiveness is the exact opposite of vengeance."[7] Forgiveness breaks the cycle of aggressive action and counter-action set up by vengeance. And in doing so, it sets us free. There is no freedom in revenge, as Arendt pointed out. *Steal my cattle, and I steal yours!* My action is not freely chosen; what I do is *dictated* by what you did and your vengeful retaliation is dictated by my reaction. Everything that follows is utterly predictable, driven by events, the opposite of freedom. By contrast, by refusing to engage in tit-for-tat revenge, I am free to act in many different ways, to make new choices. And by refusing to be trapped in the predictable cycle of revenge, my forgiveness sets you free, too, to choose a new and better path.

Meet what is worst in your enemy with what is best in you. Let his or her wrongdoing bring out the best in you. And what is best in you is not born of retaliation or hate, but of compassion and forgiveness. What is best in you is that which preserves your humanity. This is the new twist we can give to the old idea of "getting our own back" on an enemy: getting back the best, and not being reduced to the worst. The Dalai Lama tells us this story:

A few years back, a Tibetan monk who had served about eighteen years in a Chinese prison in Tibet came to see me after his escape to India. I knew him from my days in Tibet and remembered last seeing him in 1959. During the course of that meeting I had asked him what he felt was the biggest threat or danger while in prison. I was amazed at his answer. It was extraordinary and inspiring. I was expecting him to say something else: instead he said that what he most feared was losing his compassion for the Chinese.[8]

For that Tibetan monk to lose his freedom was a great loss. But to lose his compassion would have been tantamount to losing his humanity. While the Chinese were responsible for taking away his freedom, he himself would have been responsible if he let go of his compassion and thus diminished his own sense of being human.

Christ and forgiveness

The value of forgiveness is increasingly recognised, today, in the secular worlds of science and politics. The power of forgiveness has long been recognised in the traditions of all the great religions of the world. Forgiveness is at the very heart of Christian belief. Hannah Arendt argued that the greatest exponent of the power of forgiveness is the founder of our faith, Jesus of Nazareth.[9]

Forgiveness is at the very heart of Jesus' ministry. Over and over again in his teaching he urges us to forgive one another, to turn the other cheek rather than trading blow for blow with an enemy – to love our enemies, even. This is an extraordinary message! But, as Martin Luther King, the great American civil rights leader, wrote: "Far from being the pious injunction of a utopian dreamer, the command to love one's enemy is an absolute necessity for our survival. Love even for our enemies is the key to the solution of the problems of our world. Jesus is not an impractical idealist; he is the practical realist."[10] The power of his gospel breaks the knee-jerk chain reaction of pain and sets us free to choose our own actions and opens up a new vision of what human relationships could be like.

Although Jesus' insight about forgiveness came in a very specific religious context, it is every bit as relevant to the secular world. The teaching of Jesus provided Martin Luther King with his political agenda for the liberation of his people. He set out his political strategy with these remarkable words:

> To our most bitter opponents we say: "We shall match your capacity to inflict suffering by our capacity to endure suffering. We shall meet your physical force with soul force. Do to us what you will, and we shall continue to love you. We cannot in all good conscience obey your unjust laws, because non-cooperation with evil is as much a moral obligation as is cooperation with good. Throw us in jail, and we shall still love you. Send your hooded perpetrators of violence into our community at the midnight hour and beat us and leave us half dead, and we shall still love you. But be assured that we will wear you down by our capacity to suffer. One day we shall win our freedom, but not only for ourselves. We shall so appeal to your heart and conscience that we shall win you in the process, and our victory will be a double victory."[11]

The practical benefits of forgiveness in human affairs are only now being scientifically researched – as we shall see in later chapters of this book. Even the spiritual benefits of forgiveness have to be rediscovered in our own time. And, as we can see from the outstanding example of Martin Luther King, the political benefits of the forgiving spirit are incalculable. In his acceptance speech of the Nobel Peace Prize Nelson Mandela paid this tribute to his great mentor:

> Let the strivings of us all prove Martin Luther King Jr to have been correct, when he said that humanity can no longer be tragically bound to the starless midnight of racism and war. Let the efforts of us all prove that he was not a mere dreamer when he spoke of the beauty of genuine brotherhood and peace being more precious than diamonds or silver or gold. Let a new age dawn![12]

Few people have contributed more to the welfare of humanity than Martin Luther King and Nelson Mandela. The source of the indomitable inner strength of both men was their extraordinary capacity to love and forgive all their enemies. As King himself had discovered: "Love is the only force capable of transforming an enemy into a friend. We never get rid of an enemy by meeting hate with hate; we get rid of an enemy by getting rid of enmity."[13]

Jesus' teaching provides the first real insight into both the practical and spiritual gifts of forgiveness. At the heart of his teaching is the idea that forgiveness is a birthright that cannot be taken away from us, if only, like Martin Luther King or Nelson Mandela, we reach out for it.

Our right to forgiveness

It is our absolute right to forgive one another, and so to act freely, rather than being trapped by the tramlines of revenge. We need not perpetuate vendettas, cycles of pain! We are not machines, locked into the mechanical responses of revenge. We are free, absolutely free to choose a better path, free to use our many gifts to find that path.

We have an absolute need to be forgiven: to be freed from the consequences of our own misdeeds and failings, freed to find new value in ourselves and our lives. There is nothing that forces us to stay trapped in the misery of self-blame or guilt because we can choose to seek, and to accept, forgiveness. Of course, human forgiveness depends on the vagaries of the human heart: not everyone from whom we seek forgiveness will be able to offer it to us. But behind human forgiveness stands divine forgiveness, the forgiveness offered to us by God: "Ask, and it will be given you; search, and you will find; knock, and the door will be opened for you. For everyone who asks receives, and everyone who searches finds, and for everyone who knocks, the door will be opened" (Matthew 7:7-8). Jesus promises us that, if we truly ask for forgiveness, God will not refuse. It is this promise of receiving, this assurance that as we seek forgiveness we will find it, that Catholics celebrate through the sacrament of reconciliation (confession), as we shall see later in this book.

Offering and receiving forgiveness are powerful processes. Both are difficult! In later chapters, we shall explore more of what it means to offer or to ask for forgiveness. We will see how it can be possible to overcome the obstacles to giving and receiving the grace of forgiveness, and how forgiveness brings healing and protection to us all. But before we move on, let's pause a while and reflect. Do we truly want forgiveness in our lives?

EXERCISE

- Centre yourself, using the techniques we learned in the previous chapter.

- Bring yourself to bodily stillness and calm.

- Now ask yourself: What would it feel like, if I truly carried no grievances or disappointments, no ill feelings or anger towards anyone, not even myself?

- Allow yourself to experience this feeling as powerfully as you can. Do you want that feeling in your life?

- Now focus again on your breathing.

- And bring yourself gently back to the world.

This technique, too, is a very old Christian form of prayer. In many ways, reflecting on what it would be like to forgive and be forgiven is the first step towards making a commitment to seek out and live those things.

Notes

1 For more information, see the Forgiveness Project website
  <http://www.theforgivenessproject.com>

2 Jim McManus, personal recollection.

3 Pope John Paul II, *Evangelium Vitae* (London: CTS, 1995), 55.

4 Stephanie Thornton, personal recollection.

5 Correspondence to the authors.

6 Seamus Heaney, *The Cure at Troy: A Version of Sophocles' Philoctetes* (New
  York: Noonday Press, 1991), 77.

7 Hannah Arendt, *The Human Condition* (Chicago: Chicago University Press,
  1998), 240.

8 Simon Wiesenthal, *The Sunflower: On the Possibilities and Limits of
  Forgiveness* (New York: Schocken Books, 1997), 130.

9 Arendt, *The Human Condition*, 238.

10 Martin Luther King, *Strength to Love* (London: Fount, 1977), 48.

11 Ibid. 54.

12 Nelson Mandela, Nobel Peace Prize acceptance speech, 10 Dec. 1993.

13 King, *Strength to Love*, 52.

3

The shape of forgiveness

"I don't like Guinness: I don't know what it is."
Advertisement for Guinness, mid twentieth century

What does it mean to forgive? What will it commit me to, to forgive those who've hurt me? What will I have to *do*, to forgive, or to be forgiven? Questions like these lurk in our minds, as we wrestle with the problem of forgiveness. What's it going to cost me, to forgive? What will I be giving up? And in a way, most importantly: Can I do that? Can I really carry it through?

In some ways, forgiveness is one of the most problematic of all human concepts. Implicitly, almost instinctively, we believe that forgiving or seeking forgiveness is the right thing to do – that, in some unfathomable way, it is good for our lives, good for our souls. And yet! And yet, we flinch from what we imagine forgiveness might mean, might demand of us.

There's a saying: "there ain't no such thing as a free lunch". The meaning is that there is a cost for everything. There is indeed a cost to forgiveness, if cost means sacrifice, or even effort. But we believe that that cost may not be what many fear it will be, and that the gain achieved by forgiveness outweighs that cost so as to make it well spent. And what great human achievement was ever gained without some sort of cost?

To live in forgiveness is an exercise in human understanding, human control, human maturity. More importantly, it is a powerful spiritual gift to the forgiver and to the forgiven. The price we must pay for this blessing is far, far less threatening than we suppose – and yet, far, far more challenging.

Wisdom of the ages[1]

So what is this thing called forgiveness? There are so many views as to what forgiveness really is, what it really entails! Different religions, different political or moral systems propose different ideas. But all agree that forgiveness is at the core of spirituality. Forgiveness lifts us beyond our animal natures and towards the transcendent, towards the nature of God.

Hinduism

Were the Hindus the first to begin exploring the importance of forgiveness in human lives? The earliest recorded prayer asking for forgiveness is in the Hindu sacred books, dating from the Vedic period, some 1,000 to 5,000 years before the birth of Christ:

> Have mercy, spare me, Mighty Lord, O Varuna,
> whatever the offence may be by which we as men
> commit against the heavenly host, when through our
> want of thought we violate thy laws, punish us not,
> O God, for that iniquity. (Rig Veda, 7:89)

Hinduism is a faith of many gods, many traditions. Some, such as the goddess Lakshmi, forgive whether or not the human offender repents, or even understands the nature of the offence. Others, such as Vishnu, forgive only when the sinner repents. Within this tradition, forgiving the unrepentant is an attribute of the divine. Mere human beings are not expected to reach this transcendent goal. If the offender is unrepentant, we mere mortals *need* not forgive.

And yet, forgiveness is a profound virtue for the Hindu faith. It is one of the keystones to the path of righteousness that can redeem a life, along with patience, forbearance, compassion. To aspire to forgive, as the gods forgive, is an important spiritual goal.

Repentance is also important for the spiritual state of the offender. The Hindu believes in reincarnation: that we live a succession of lives, each reflecting the karma of the previous life – the law of cause and effect. Evil done in this life *and unrepented* will be worked through in a subsequent incarnation. To enjoy a happy reincarnation one must not only embrace the neutral virtue of avoiding evil, but also embrace the positive virtues – of compassion, patience, forbearance, forgiveness. In sum, one must aspire to the transcendental nature of the gods.

Buddhism

Uniquely among the major religions of the world, Buddhism is not based on a belief in the existence of a higher power, a god. Nor is there any one word for "forgiveness" in the Buddhist tradition. Nevertheless, forgiveness is at the heart of two key concepts for Buddhism: forbearance and compassion.

For the Buddhist, forbearance embraces both stoically enduring an offence committed against one, and also renouncing the rage and resentment that such an assault might engender. The idea of endurance adds a new dimension to forgiveness: survival, the preservation of self, despite attack. This goes beyond the basic notion of forgiveness as a matter of renouncing resentment. Forgiveness becomes a positive, constructive thing, a matter of self-preservation rather than just a letting go. Compassion, in the Buddhist tradition, helps the person to think differently about the offender:

> Compassion and pity as Buddhist virtues effect a change in attitude by which the offender is no longer thought of as such. Instead, through compassion and pity, one ideally comes to empathise with the suffering of the offender, and one then takes steps to ease the suffering, even though both empathy and the action taken to relive suffering are undeserved.[2]

Thus one empathises with the criminal on his or her way to execution and feels pity for him or her. In the Buddhist tradition "the truly compassionate take pity even on their would-be murderers".[3]

Compassion seeks to ease the suffering of others; forbearance seeks not to inflict suffering by any form of retaliation. Resentment, the opposite of forgiveness, can lead nowhere, can never be satisfied. Some of the sayings of the Buddha underline this:

> In those who harbour such thoughts: "He reviled
> me, he beat me, he overpowered me, he robbed me",
> anger is never stilled ... Hatred never ceases by
> hatred in this world. Through loving kindness it comes
> to an end. This is an ancient Law.

and this:

> Just as fire, however fierce, is quenched when
> it meets a large river brimful of water, so a raging
> heart grows calm if one inclines to forbearance, the
> mainstay in this life and in the next. Practice forbearance
> and you will avoid evil by cutting it off at the root.
> The result will be that you will arouse no ill feeling
> because of your friendly disposition. You will be loved
> and honoured for it and thereby win happiness.[4]

Compassion and forbearance are at the very heart of the Buddhist spirituality. These virtues do not depend on the repentance of the offender. In fact, forbearance is the way in which one deals with lack of repentance. It is forbearance that makes it possible for the person to have compassion even for the offender. In a sense, compassion implies a degree of reconciliation between victim and offender – since, through compassion, the victim re-endorses the human worth of the offender. But this "reconciliation" is spiritual rather than anything else. It does not require any degree of reciprocation on the part of the offender, nor the establishment of any relationship between offender and victim.

The Abrahamic religions

Forgiveness is a complex matter for all the so-called "Abrahamic" religions: Judaism, Christianity and Islam. Is the God of Abraham a forgiving God? So many fundamentalists – Jewish, Christian, Muslim – seem to have believed *not*, citing sacred scripture as an excuse for the bestial murder of religious opponents: the brutality of the Crusades; a self-defence that meets stone-throwing children with machine guns; an opposition to liberal, capitalist values expressed by suicide bombers. Indeed, there are texts that, taken completely out of context, *might* legitimise the bad behaviour of Abraham's descendants. But overall, the sacred texts of Judaism, Christianity and Islam are clear: vengeful violence is as unacceptable as any other violence. Forgiveness is a virtue, and an important one at that. Spiritual growth is a matter of becoming God-like. And God, in all three traditions, is forgiving!

1. Judaism

Judaism is the oldest, albeit the smallest of the Abrahamic traditions. Throughout the Hebrew scriptures, there is a constant theme of a forgiving God. And this is the ultimate reason why Jews, through their long history, have tried to practise forgiveness. For the Jew, the ultimate path to God and to a strong spirituality is to "walk in his ways" (Deuteronomy 28:9), in other words, to imitate God. As scripture says: "The LORD, the LORD, a God merciful and gracious, slow to anger, and abounding in steadfast love and faithfulness, keeping steadfast love for the thousandth generation, forgiving iniquity and transgression and sin" (Exodus 34:6-7); and, "The Lord is just in all his ways, and kind in all his doings" (Psalm 145:17).

The first compilation of Jewish law, the Mishnah, states that an offender must make reparations to his or her victim, but that this is not enough to earn God's forgiveness. For that, the offender must ask the victim for forgiveness and, in Jewish tradition, the victim is obliged to forgive if he or she is asked to do so: to refuse three times would make the victim a sinner. But one is not obliged to forgive those who do not ask for forgiveness. Jewish tradition doesn't look favourably on forgiving those who haven't repented in any way: a victim may forgive the unrepentant out of charity, but he or she is not obliged to forgive out of justice. Withholding forgiveness until the offender repents and asks for pardon is believed, in Jewish tradition, to be ultimately best for the offender: it ties the blessing of forgiveness to the moment of conversion away from evil deeds, so providing the best start to new spiritual growth in the offender.

2. Islam

One of the ninety-nine attributes of Allah is "The Forgiving One". Like Jews, Muslims strive to forgive because Allah forgives. The Qur'an says "pardon [your] fellow men because God loves the doers of good" (3:134); and: "Keep to forgiveness, and enjoin kindness." (7:199)

For the Muslim, forgiveness does not require the repentance of the offender. It is a grace that the victim is free to offer, whether the offender repents or not, although repentance makes reconciliation between offender and victim possible. Reconciliation between human offender and victim is a desirable thing – but it is not essential, and the Islamic faith recognises that it may not always be either possible or advisable. Forgiveness is a grace in and of itself, bringing great reward from Allah. Indeed, humbly seeking forgiveness for one's own transgressions and magnanimously forgiving others for theirs are the essential prerequisites for seeking the greatest of all rewards: forgiveness from Allah.

3. Christianity

Forgiveness is a central theme of Jesus' teaching, a core pillar on which Christianity rests. Indeed, some (such as the Jewish philosopher Hannah Arendt) believe that Jesus was the greatest exponent of forgiveness, the first to realise the full power of forgiveness in human lives and spirituality.

Both Judaism and Islam allow a victim to extract an equitable revenge (an eye for an eye) – though both faiths see forgiveness as more virtuous, more in keeping with the ways of God. But Christ advocated a pure forgiveness, a forgiveness that never seeks revenge, is not conditional on the repentance of the offender, and is offered over and over again. We are to forgive "Not seven times, but, I tell you, seventy-seven times." Notice that Jesus' "seventy-seven times" is the exact opposite of Lamech's demand for "seventy-sevenfold" vengeance (Genesis 4:24).

The route to spirituality

Across all the great religions of the world, there is substantial agreement: forgiveness is a virtue that brings us closer to spiritual health, or to God. We forgive because forgiveness has in it a spark of divinity, and, in forgiving, we walk in the ways of the Divine. We forgive also because we ourselves need forgiveness, because we need to receive that forgiveness from God. For most of the great religious traditions forgiveness is unconditional: repentance on the part of the offender and reconciliation between offender and victim may be desirable, but they are not essential. Forgiveness stands alone.

Let's look in more detail at the divine dimension of forgiveness. For Christians, forgiveness is the route to union with God. Our forgiving of one another is the only human activity mentioned in the Lord's Prayer. In St Matthew's version we say, "forgive us our debts, as we also have forgiven our debtors" (Matthew 6:12). Jesus concludes his teaching on forgiveness in this section of the Gospel with the words, "For if you forgive others their trespasses, your heavenly Father will also forgive you; but if you do not forgive others, neither will your Father forgive your trespasses" (Matthew 6:14-15). "By this combination of conditional statements, Matthew could hardly put it more emphatically that human forgiveness is a necessary condition for divine forgiveness."[5]

To understand the nature of this relationship between human and divine forgiveness we have to go to chapter eighteen in Matthew's Gospel. In this chapter we have the parable of the "unforgiving servant" who owes the king such an enormous sum of money that he could never possibly pay it back, so he pleads for mercy. The king graciously pardons his debt. Then, walking away in his new-found freedom from debt, he meets a fellow servant who, in turn, owes him a paltry sum and demands repayment. The fellow servant pleads for mercy, but he refuses and has the man imprisoned. The other servants report all this to the king who is furious. He calls in the unforgiving servant, whom he had forgiven, and withdraws his forgiveness: "You wicked slave! I forgave you all that debt because you pleaded with me. Should you not have had mercy on your fellow slave, as I had mercy on you?" (Matthew 18:32-33). This parable has three scenes which Christians have pondered for centuries:

- 1st scene: the servant who owes the unpayable debt pleads for more time and the king forgives the whole debt.

- 2nd scene: the forgiven servant, now released from such a burden of debt, meets a fellow servant who owes him a small sum and who pleads for more time. But the forgiven servant has him thrown into prison.

- 3rd scene: the king responds in kind to the unforgiving servant and has him thrown into prison.

The unforgiving servant now learns the meaning of "forgive us as we have forgiven them". The king forgave the servant without first ensuring that the servant would forgive fellow servants. The king's forgiveness was meant to be unconditional. The condition came in as the servant responded to that forgiveness. Rather than letting it flow through him to others, he withheld forgiveness and in so doing lost it himself.

In Christian forgiveness, the divine forgiveness comes first. Even before we turn to God in prayer to ask for forgiveness, that forgiveness is already being offered. All we have to do is accept it. In truly accepting divine forgiveness, we should experience a conversion that opens our hearts to share what we have received. Without this desire to share there has been no conversion, no acceptance of God's forgiveness, and so divine forgiveness cannot be retained.

In Mark's Gospel Jesus says: "whatever you ask for in prayer, believe that you have received it, and it will be yours. Whenever you stand praying, forgive, if you have anything against anyone; so that your Father in heaven may also forgive you your trespasses" (Mark 11:24-25). Jesus is insisting that we cannot stand in the presence of God, asking God to forgive us, if we are refusing to forgive others. And notice that Mark simply says "forgive, if you have anything against anyone" – no mention of the person's repentance or apology.

Jesus practised this kind of forgiveness himself. On the cross he prayed for his executioners, "Father, forgive them; for they do not know what they are doing" (Luke 23:34). His forgiveness of them did not depend on their repentance, but without repentance his generosity would not change their hearts. As the theologian Gregory Jones writes, "Those who are forgiven by Jesus are called to embody that forgiven-ness in the new life signified by communion with Jesus and with other disciples. Indeed that forgiven-ness calls believers to live penitent lives that seek to reconstruct human relationships in the service of holiness of heart and life."[6]

Filled with God's love and with God's Spirit, we are moved to offer to others what God has given us: unconditional forgiveness. Forgiveness is the work of the Spirit. Christ's forgiveness comes to us in the Spirit and our forgiveness of others goes to them in the Spirit. St Paul says: "If we live by the Spirit, let us also be guided by the Spirit" (Galatians 5:25).

Thus for the Christian, forgiveness is a mark of our reconciliation with God. But forgiveness itself does not require reconciliation between offender and victim, since it can be offered to the unrepentant as much as the repentant.

The nature of forgiveness

Having begun to explore the divine dimension, let's look again at the human experience of forgiveness. What does it demand of us, what will it cost us? What will we gain from forgiving, or from being forgiven? What will I have to do to forgive or be forgiven?

Forgiveness is not…forgetting

A great deal of the difficulty we have with the idea of forgiveness comes from the saying, "forgive and forget". We human beings are capable of forgetting a very great deal. But we are not capable of forgetting everything – and nor is it in our real interests to do so. Can a mother forget that her child has been murdered? Can an abandoned wife forget that her husband has left her? Can a nation forget that terrorists have bombed its cities, or that another nation has tried to exterminate its people through genocide? Can I even forget that such-and-such a neighbour has attacked my reputation, or that a colleague has undermined my work? Can I, for that matter, simply forget how badly I behaved to this or that person?

None of these things is forgettable, and indeed, none of them should be forgotten. These things happened, and the fact needs to be honoured in our memories. Furthermore, we need to learn from our experience and our mistakes; such learning would not be possible if we could simply wipe those experiences and those mistakes from our minds.

Forgiveness is… about coming to terms with reality

However unforgettable an event, it can be forgiven. Perhaps we should not say "that's unforgivable" but "that's unforgettable". In fact even terrible things *must* be forgiven if we are to move on and live healthy lives. To refuse to forgive is to refuse to let go of pain, resentment, grievance – the status of a victim. Much misery and mental malaise are caused by the refusal to let go of our grievances and pain. If we cannot let go of those things we will be trapped for ever in the past, for ever the victim of those who have attacked us, or of our own bad behaviour. Forgiveness is not about forgetting, but it is about coming to terms with what has happened, what cannot be undone, incorporating it into our lives and moving on. Rather than saying, "forgive and forget", we should say, "forgive and move on". Forgiveness allows us to remember without bitterness, even if sadness never fades.

Forgiveness does not... let the offender "off the hook"
In forgiving those who harm us we neither tolerate nor condone the offence. Quite the reverse; how could we forgive without first acknowledging that there is something to be forgiven, that those we forgive have done something wrong? Criticism of the wrong done to us is necessarily inherent in the act of forgiveness.

Forgiveness is an active thing, a positive naming of the wrong done to us and a clear declaration that it was wrong. This is very different from "turning a blind eye" and letting the wrongdoer continue as if nothing had happened. It is very different from finding some way of pretending that the wrongdoing was somehow not so bad, and thereby condoning it. True forgiveness confronts the reality of the wrongdoing and deals with it honestly.

Nor does forgiveness mean that we must "write off" the offence, providing a pardon to the offender. Each of us is responsible for our actions, and must face the consequences of those actions. Each of us lives in a complex social system which imposes obligations upon us, obligations to behave according to certain standards. Forgiveness does not take the offender outside that system – in fact, it could not. Forgiveness is an emotion in the individual heart, bearing on the emotional health and spiritual strength of the individual, quite separate from the collective will that imposes social laws. Complete forgiveness for the offender does not undermine your right to whatever legal redress is appropriate for the wrong done to you. For example, Pope John Paul II forgave the Turkish terrorist Mehmet Ali Ağca for trying to kill him, visiting him in prison to do so. But the Pope did not ask for Mehmet's release from prison. Forgiveness is the gift of the individual. Imprisonment was the price demanded by society for Mehmet's actions.

Forgiveness... sets the victim free
Forgiveness in no way lets the offender get away with his or her wrongdoing. Rather, it is the victim of wrongdoing who is set free through forgiveness.

When we are attacked, we suffer. We suffer on many levels: our view of the world may be profoundly changed, our confidence undermined. We may harbour fear and hurt – outrage that another human being could treat us like this. We may harbour hate, frustration, a thirst to hurt another as we have been hurt. All of these things are natural responses of victimhood, and all are what make the state of victimhood so very damaging.

We don't have to accept that state of victimhood. Instead, we can assert our own individuality, our own spiritual values and strength, and refuse to be made into a victim. This is the power of forgiveness: in forgiving, all the negative feelings of the victim are stripped away.

Forgiveness brings healing at every level: healing of the body, as damaging physiological tensions drain away; healing of the mind, as constructive thoughts replace destructive ones, and healing of the spirit, as we transcend the evil that has been done to us.

Forgiveness is not... reconciliation

Many people believe that to say that they have truly forgiven someone, they must be reconciled with that individual and re-engage in a relationship. This is a mistake and can be a serious obstacle to the desire to forgive.

Reconciliation implies a renewed relationship between victim and offender. In an ideal world, perhaps forgiveness would lead to reconciliation. But the world is far from ideal. Some offenders are unwilling or unable to repent of their bad behaviour – some are unable even to recognise the impact of what they have done. Reconciliation with the unrepentant may be dangerous, or even impossible. And even where there is repentance, reconciliation may not be a healthy option, where memories of the past are unforgettable, or where the personality of those concerned will create a continuing problem. Furthermore, an offender may refuse reconciliation, even when it is offered. There is nothing the forgiver can do about this.

Forgiveness does not demand that we expose ourselves to further pain in any way, nor that we take responsibility for another's actions, and so does not require reconciliation. This is acknowledged in all the major religions of the world.

Forgiveness is... strength

Forgiveness is not the easy option. It is seldom the immediate response of the human heart to forgive an attacker. Revenge seems so much more attractive! And then there is the tendency to self-pity, to display our wounds in accusation, nurse our sense of injustice.

In striving to rise above the urge for vengeance, and in letting go of our claim for pity, we must set aside powerful human emotions. This is the cost, the sacrifice of forgiveness, and it takes courage, commitment and strength. It may also take considerable effort, effort towards empathy with the offender, towards a constructive perspective on the world as it is now, after the offence, effort to come to terms with grief for the world that existed beforehand.

Forgiveness… cannot be a moral duty imposed upon us

For all that religion exhorts us to forgive, forgiving is not a moral obligation imposed on us from without. In fact, offering forgiveness as a moral duty can be difficult and damaging. Believing that I *must* forgive you, I may be tempted to offer a very inferior form of forgiveness. I may offer no more than the formalities of forgiveness, the words "I forgive you." These are empty words, unless they reflect the urge of our own heart to forgive, an urge that needs deeper roots than duty.

Many of us have, at one time or another, told someone that we forgive them, knowing that forgiving is the right thing to do or being pressured to forgive by others, but knowing in our hearts that we have *not* truly forgiven the other. Such false forgiveness can be damaging to the "forgiver", driving powerful feelings underground to fester and bringing scant relief from the negativity of grievance and resentment. False forgiveness can be damaging to the "forgiven" too, creating a world of mixed messages and false reconciliation, where what poses as compassion masks subtle attacks.

True forgiveness springs from the individual, and cannot be imposed from outside. True forgiveness reflects the personal qualities and strength of the forgiver, things that cannot be commanded by anyone else, nor by a religious injunction. True forgiveness is a life-giving right that no one can take away from us, rather than a burden of duty imposed upon us. Only true forgiveness sets us free.

Forgiveness… stems from the decision to forgive

It is our inalienable human right to forgive. It is our inalienable right to let go of pain and grief, to let go of hate and grievance, to let go of suffering. We are not obliged to carry those things through the rest of our lives just because someone has injured us! The grace of forgiveness brings healing and wholeness to those who forgive. We have an absolute right to that healing. No one should be allowed to rob us of that. If someone has injured us, we have the right not to let that injury poison the rest of our lives.

The psychologist Gerald Jampolsky writes: "From the perspective of Love and Spirit, forgiveness is the willingness to let go of the hurtful past. It is the *decision* to no longer suffer, to heal your heart and soul. It is the *choice* to no longer find value in hatred or anger. And it is *letting go* of the desire to hurt others or ourselves because of something that is already in the past. It is *willingness* to open our eyes to the light in other people rather than to judge or condemn them" (italics added).[7] This emphasis on choice and decision finds an echo in the work of psychologists Robert Enright and John North: "Forgiveness is a willingness to abandon one's right to resentment, negative judgment, and indifferent behaviour toward one who unjustly injured us, while fostering the undeserved qualities of compassion, generosity, and even love toward him or her."[8]

Forgiveness begins with the willingness to forgive. At first, there may be no more than the desire to forgive, or even the wish that we could imagine forgiveness. This wish for forgiveness opens the door for us to discover how to forgive. Without it, true forgiveness isn't possible.

Living examples
Forgiveness is a gift all of us can choose to give, or to receive. Far too few of us reach out for that gift. But some do, some do. And when we encounter those who forgive, we can be powerfully moved.

Take the case of Marie Fatayi-Williams, a Nigerian Catholic married to a Muslim. Her son Anthony was one of those killed in the terrorist attack on London on 7 July 2005, blown to bits as he travelled to work. She flew to London when her son went missing. On 22 July, a scant few days later, she was interviewed on the radio. Movingly, she described her pain and grief for Anthony, her firstborn child and only son. Listening to her account of her fear on hearing of the bombings – her dread as time passed and Anthony made no contact, her cry of need to hear from him, to hold him, to touch him – it was impossible not to share the horror and desolation of the moment, the magnitude of her loss. Her words were universal words of suffering. But then, extraordinarily, she described her sorrow for the bomber who had been driven to such a desperate act, and for the community that bred him. This highly intelligent woman could make no sense of what had happened – it seemed utterly senseless. But her faith in God was absolute. God brings good out of evil. The evil deed that destroyed her son would not have the last word on his life! Only two weeks after her son's death she began setting up a peace foundation in Anthony's name – The Anthony Fatayi-Williams Foundation for Peace and Conflict Resolution – to promote understanding and love in our multicultural community. For this woman, rage and revenge are pointless: nothing will bring back her adored son. Nothing will heal his mutilated body. The only way forward is to forgive, and to work to make some good grow from this bitter soil.

Listening to this interview was a humbling experience; how little I have to forgive, by comparison! How far short of her ideal of forgiveness I fall, even for my far lesser hurts! But listening to the interview was also an exalting experience: the working of the Holy Spirit is so very clear in this brave woman. How gloriously a human being can rise to spiritual challenge! How amazing to be a human being, myself possessed of the potential to fulfil that glory!

EXERCISE

- Centre yourself, using the techniques we learned in the first chapter of this book.

- Bring yourself to bodily stillness and calm.

- Now ask yourself: How honest is my desire for forgiveness? How strong? Why do I want forgiveness? What does forgiveness mean to me?

- Now focus again on your breathing.

- And bring yourself gently back to the world.

Forgiveness begins with the true desire to forgive. Recognising and understanding that desire in ourselves opens the door for the Holy Spirit to work in us, bringing the grace of forgiveness.

Notes

1   The material in this section is based closely on the excellent interviews with leaders of each of the great world religions reported in Mark Rye et al., "Religious Perspectives on Forgiveness", M.E. in McCullough, K.I. Pargament and C.E. Thoresen (eds), *Forgiveness: Theory, Research and Practice* (London: Guilford Press, 2000).

2   Ibid. 22.

3   Ibid.

4   From the Dhammapada, as quoted in Rye et al., 27 (see n. 1).

5   Todd Pokifka-Joe, "Probing the Relationship between Divine and Human Forgiveness in Matthew", in Alistair McFadyen and Marcel Sarot (eds), *Forgiveness and Truth* (Edinburgh: T & T Clark, 2001), 167.

6   Gregory Jones, *Embodying Forgiveness: A Theological Analysis* (Grand Rapids, MI: W. B. Eerdmans, 1995), 121.

7   Gerald Jampolsky MD, *Forgiveness: The Greatest Healer of All* (Hillsboro, OR: Beyond Words, 1999), 17.

8   Robert Enright and John North (eds), *Exploring Forgiveness* (Madison: University of Wisconsin Press, 1998), 26.

4

Science and forgiveness

"The stupid neither forgive nor forget; the naive forgive and forget;
the wise forgive but do not forget."
Thomas Szasz, 1973, *The Second Sin*

We have seen that every great world religion believes that forgiveness is a good thing: that it is good for the individual who forgives or who is forgiven, that self-forgiveness is healing, that forgiveness has beneficial effects for society as a whole, and that feeling forgiven by God is the most healing thing of all. Do these claims stand up to inspection? Is there scientific evidence to support them?

Science had not paid all that much attention to forgiveness until very recently. Only in the past twenty-five years has the topic even begun to be researched. Even now, the majority of students training in psychology will not be taught much about forgiveness – even though the evidence is, increasingly, that forgiveness is an important factor in psychological health.

How can it be that science, so very much dominated by so-called "Western" culture over the past centuries, has paid so very little attention to forgiveness, when that same Western culture was profoundly shaped and formed by Christianity – a faith that placed forgiveness at the very heart of life?

Perhaps the neglect of forgiveness in science reflects, to some degree, the historical tendency for science and religion to view one another with suspicion and to reject one another's great insights. Happily this historic tendency is fading. Today there is increasing recognition that science and religion have valuable insights to offer – and that these insights are surprisingly in tune with one another. Here, we examine what science can see: the benefits to mind and body.

Letting go of negativity: why me?

Across all religions and cultures, the heart of forgiveness is a matter of letting go of negativity. In forgiving, we undergo a benevolent change in our attitudes and intentions towards our enemies and transgressors, a change that involves a willingness to let go of resentment and grievance and revenge. Strangely, this definition of forgiveness means that the one who must change is the victim, the one who has been offended. It is he or she who must let go of negativity. Many people will bridle at that idea. Already, I am the victim of injustice! Must I now be the one to change? How can that be healing? How can that be fair?

But yet, the evidence suggests that those who forgive are blessed: immediately, there are benefits to the body. Immediately, also, there are benefits to the mind. These things are the realm of science, and are our focus here.

Why should I forgive, when I am the victim?

If you treat me badly, steal my possessions, maybe even physically attack me, surely it is *you* who ought to change, *you* who ought to be thrust out of your habitual orbit and forced to come to some new position? Why should I change? Why should I forgive you?

When someone harms us, what can we do? We can protest at the injustice of it, we can try to recover what we have lost – but often, these things will not be possible. And what then?

> A while back someone stole my wallet and all my credit cards, cash, driver's licence and so on. It created a terrible problem! I had to cancel all the cards. For nearly a week, until the replacements came, I had no money and no means of getting any. I had to borrow money to get the car out of the car park on the day of the theft, and had to rely on friends for food until the new cards came through! Then there were weeks waiting anxiously to see whether someone would use the driver's licence to steal my

identity and run up debts in my name. Worst of all was the loss of photos of my son, taken twenty years ago when he was a baby, and the very first letter he had written to me when he was five years old, and other irreplaceable souvenirs I carried everywhere. I was surprised how wounded and vulnerable I felt, knowing that someone else had those things. The police didn't catch the thief, and I didn't get my things back.

I was very glad to know Jim [McManus] when this happened, and for all his wise teaching in our discussions of forgiveness. What good would catching the thief or putting him in prison do me? He'd have long ago thrown away my precious letter and photos. My loss can't be undone. And even if I knew who he was, stealing something of his wouldn't help me, nor any other sort of revenge – I'd end up feeling soiled, and wouldn't be any nearer my lost treasures for it. As Jim pointed out, there were only two real choices for me in this situation: either to brood on my loss and the unfairness, the wrongness of it, hassling the police to search harder and imagining revenge – a very stressful choice; or to let go of my distress somehow. I can't do that by pretending that losing those irreplaceable childhood treasures doesn't matter or doesn't hurt – it does, and I'll never convince myself otherwise. I can only accept that the theft happened and let go of my resentment, my desire for revenge, to "do something about it". And that, in essence, means forgiving.[1]

Unforgiveness generally has no effect on the transgressor. But it harms the one who cannot forgive, trapping him or her in the pain of the moment. Forgiveness sets the victim free. And in so doing, it has powerful benefits for mind and body.

Forgiveness heals
The general belief in every religious tradition and our common sense tells us that forgiveness is healing. How could it be otherwise?

And indeed, research is rapidly showing that forgiveness is an intrinsically healing experience. Those who can forgive, those who can accept forgiveness are healthier in both mind and body than those who cannot.

For example, Mark Rye and his colleagues found that divorced men and women who could forgive their ex-spouse were mentally healthier than those who could not. Those who could let go of negative perceptions, feelings and intentions towards the former spouse were less depressed, calmer, and reported a higher level of existential wellbeing than those who could not.[2]

In another study, Janette Taylor found that forgiving the partners who had attacked them was a key element contributing to healing and recovery among women who had experienced domestic violence and went on to *thrive* – physically, mentally and socially – rather than merely surviving.[3]

In therapeutic contexts, too, it is increasingly found that forgiveness is a core part of the process of healing deep hurts and transforming unhealthy life stories and psychological states into healthy ones.[4] For example, working with a group of Irish women, all of whom had lost sons or husbands through the violence in Northern Ireland, Dr Fred Luskin found that the levels of stress and of emotional pain these women brought to his programme fell dramatically as they worked on forgiveness, ending the week's course at less than half the level that had been typical at the start. These improvements were still evident six months later.[5]

The evidence is mounting up that forgiveness is good for the mind and body. And indeed, it isn't hard to see why forgiving is better for us than refusing to forgive.

Forgiveness and the body
The negativity that goes with unforgiveness is stressful. As we brood on the wrongs done to us, our sense of outrage and feelings of

grievance increase. We imagine courses of action we might take in revenge, and our hearts beat faster, our adrenalin pumps. This physiological stress isn't good for us. Sustained for long enough, it damages the body, making vital organs work harder, blood pressure rise and so on. Anything that calms us and reduces this physiological stress is beneficial. Researchers such as Andrew Newberg believe that this may be the first key to how forgiveness heals: at the heart of forgiveness is the process of letting go of the feelings and perceptions that fuel physiological stress.[6]

Indeed, studies of the physiological effects of forgiveness support this idea. For example, Fred Luskin found that when college students brooded on a wrong, rehearsing a grudge against the offender, their blood pressure, heart rate and muscle tension rose – whereas when these students imagined forgiving the offender their bodily systems returned to a healthy state. Thus both forgiveness and unforgiveness have a clear effect on the body, an effect that is experienced as positive in the case of forgiveness and negative in the case of unforgiveness.[7]

Forgiveness and mental health
Brooding over grievances, harbouring negativity towards ourselves and others, is damaging at a psychological level as well as a physiological one.

Research by the psychologist Susan Nolen-Hoeksema shows that churning the same thing around in our minds, feeding our sense of grievance or helplessness, is a major factor in unhappiness and ill mental health of many kinds.[8] As we brood on hurts and grievances we become depressed, and we feel hopeless and helpless. Our self-esteem seeps away, and we tend to see ourselves as damaged, powerless victims. We trap ourselves in a rut, endlessly reliving the wrong in our minds, even exaggerating it.

Forgiveness sets us free from this pattern of negative brooding and rumination. It sets us free to move on, to heal and be happy again – free to find new and more constructive things to think about and so to grow and enrich our lives rather than being stuck reliving the past. As we focus on new and more constructive things, our perception of ourselves as *victims* seeps away, to be replaced by a healthier self-esteem.

Clinicians have long believed in these benefits of forgiveness. Robert Enright has now provided very clear evidence that the effects are real. He has shown that forgiving has direct effects in decreasing anxiety and depression and improving self-esteem. Indeed, it has been said that Enright's evidence shows that forgiveness may be "as important to the treatment of emotional and mental disorders as ... sulpha drugs and penicillin have been to the treatment of infectious diseases".[9]

Forgiveness and society

Furthermore, it turns out that there are social benefits associated with forgiving: those who forgive elicit an upsurge of warm feelings and empathy in those around them. The aggression of an enemy is defused by being offered forgiveness, which often heads off further attacks.[10] In Rwanda, after the genocide, counselling oriented towards forgiveness produced better social relations and less continuing violence than anything else.[11] Being seen to be forgiving can improve an individual's social status and integration in society – both of which are conducive to better mental and physical health.

Forgiving and being forgiven

Many of the benefits of forgiving also apply to being forgiven, and for the same reasons. It's a stressful thing, to feel oneself the object of hatred or rage, to be judged and cast off as a villain, bad. Like the unforgiving, the unforgiven can suffer serious physiological stress, as well as the constant pressure of criticism and social rejection, and the low self-esteem that goes with those things. Being forgiven removes the stress and reinstates us as acceptable, adequate.

As healing as it is to be forgiven by other people, self-forgiveness is probably the most important factor of all for mental health. When we are unforgiving towards ourselves, endlessly blaming ourselves for mistakes or bad deeds, subjecting ourselves to a constant stream of self-criticism, we can punish ourselves more relentlessly, more cruelly, more consistently than anyone else ever could. To refuse to forgive myself condemns me to a living hell of anxiety, depression, stress and self-rejection. Self-forgiveness is the essential first step towards mental health and self-esteem.

Psychology and forgiveness

The heart of forgiveness is a benevolent change in intentions, attitudes and emotions towards a wrongdoer. In forgiving, we let go of the grievance, resentment, hate or fear we might have felt for the transgressor; we let go of any intention of seeking revenge or harming the wrongdoer; we cease to demonise him or her.

In being forgiven we accept a new appraisal of our value in the eyes of those we have wounded, a new situation free from the risk of retaliation or opprobrium. And in embracing forgiveness, we are blessed with healing in mind and body.

There is much that psychology can tell us about how this process of forgiveness happens. It is not the same in every individual. For some, forgiveness is very rapid – a sudden transformation. For others, it's a long, hard process. Some individuals refuse to forgive altogether, hanging on to their grievances, nursing them, fanning the flames of negativity, orienting their whole lives around hate-filled unforgiveness directed at transgressors, misfortunes, themselves or God.[12] Which of these paths an individual will most easily follow reflects many things, including personality, maturity and circumstance.

Personality and forgiveness

Human personality is harder to describe than you might think. Dozens of different theories about what personality is and how it influences our lives have been put forward over the past hundred years. Gradually, a consensus is developing that personality has three distinct components: traits, strategies and life stories.

There seem to be five main traits that characterise human personality: openness to experience, conscientiousness, extraversion, agreeableness and neuroticism (O.C.E.A.N.).[13] These five traits may well be determined in large part by our genes, and be relatively constant throughout our lives.[14] In some senses our basic personality traits are what we bring to any situation. Obviously, an individual who is neurotic and disagreeable will have a tendency to react quite differently to many things from the way a more stable and agreeable person would react, and such differences may influence whether a given individual is more or less readily disposed to be forgiving.

Do our inborn personality traits determine our capacity for forgiveness? No. These traits may well be the least important influence on forgiveness[15] – which is just as well, since traits are not very changeable. Far more important to the tendency to forgive are the goals and projects we focus on, and the life-story we tell to make sense of our personal history.

Each of us, at any one time in our lives, has projects that we hold dear, goals that we would like to achieve (finishing writing this book on time, for example!). These goals vary from the large goals that powerfully structure our lives (being a priest or a psychologist, for instance) to the more mundane – getting the garden in order, or raising funds for a project. Whatever their level, the goals we hold dear and the strategies we use to try to achieve these goals define our lives and personalities. As we pass through life, we weave our experiences, our hopes and fears, our fortunes and misfortunes into a coherent story, giving meaning and personal significance to events. The stories we tell about ourselves, the projects we hold dear and the strategies we use to try to achieve them change far more than do our "scores" on the five core traits: we change our aspirations and plans to reflect events, change the meanings we give to our experiences to reflect growing maturity.

At any one time, the goals we care about, and the story we believe about ourselves, affect how we respond to setbacks or attacks from a wrongdoer. For example, here are two very different stories about a woman dealing with the personal trauma of being infected with HIV/AIDS:

Version 1

Mary now accepted the fact that she had HIV, much as she accepted the fact that some of her physical features weren't exactly perfect. Yes, probably some of her actions had contributed to her getting HIV in the first place. But she had stopped blaming herself for these past mistakes. Whatever happened, whatever she had done or not done – there was no way to change those things. She accepted this, and felt a kind of peace about it now. Anyway, Mary thought, her imperfections were a part of herself, who she was as a person. What matters is the whole picture, imperfections and all, and what you do with that. Mary felt good about the whole picture of herself.

Version 2

Mary thought constantly about what she could have done differently so that she didn't end up getting HIV. "If only I had not done this … if only I had done that …" were thoughts that ran through her head, especially at night. She blamed herself for what she did – and didn't do. She also blamed herself for who she was. If she had been a different person, this wouldn't have happened to her. But deep down, Mary felt that she could never change who she was, and that basically, she wasn't a very good person. No wonder she got HIV – she deserved this terrible disease, much as she deserved the other bad things that had happened to her in life.[16]

These two different perspectives are two different ways of interpreting and giving meaning to the same misfortune. It's easy to see how the first life-story provides the basis for Mary to forgive herself and make the best of her situation – whereas the second life-story traps her in self-blame and despair. The story we tell ourselves about our lives is affected by many things, from our knowledge of the world to our religious beliefs, the maturity of our reasoning or experience. Life-stories can be rewritten – through therapy, through advice from friends, or through rethinking things for ourselves. Hard work though this can be, it means that forgiveness is open to all types of personality, even if some start better equipped for forgiveness than others.

Forgiveness and maturity

If forgiveness reflects our personalities and the life-stories we tell ourselves, it also reflects our developmental maturity and the way we think about and understand the world. Pioneering work in this field by Enright shows that how we forgive relates to developmental stages in how we understand morality as a whole.[17]

For the young child, morality is at first a matter of authority and punishment. The reason for "being good" is simply in order not to be punished by an authority figure who imposes absolute rules. Enright found that, at this first stage, the child believes that wrongs must be punished – and forgiveness is possible only where a suitable revenge has been taken. For example, *I'll forgive you when I've got my own back on you.*

Enright found that children, by about nine or ten years of age, had reached the second stage of understanding. Morality is a matter of reciprocity between individuals rather than absolute authority: it's only fair that I treat you as you treat me. From this point of view, I can forgive you if you make things up to me, restoring the balance of our relationship. I needn't exact revenge. For example, *I'll forgive you if you make it up to me somehow, so we're still friends.*

By age fifteen or sixteen, the average adolescent has reached stage three of moral reasoning: what is good or right is less a matter of authoritative rules or personal reciprocity and more a matter of "being a good person" as society defines that – in other words, doing what is expected of one. If society expects me to forgive you, then I must do that, to be a good person, whether or not you have been punished or have offered any sort of apology or restitution. For example, *I'll forgive you because I'm a good person.*

College students have usually grown beyond this rather fuzzy desire to be good, developing theories about what makes society tick and what makes an action moral or immoral. These theories might fit closely with the views of their immediate community – or might be quite different, reflecting their broader experience or education. At this stage, forgiveness depends on what the individual's philosophy of life or religion demands, regardless of what other people might think, and regardless of whether or not the transgressor has been punished or has offered restitution. For example, *I'll forgive you because I'm a Christian, and that's what Christians do.*

Although Enright describes these four stages of reasoning about morality and forgiveness as typical of the given age groups, many individuals of any given age think about these things in ways typical of a younger age group. Some adults have not progressed beyond the reasoning typical of the young child. Most adults have made little progress beyond the reasoning typical of the college student. And yet, there are two higher stages of reasoning than these initial four.

The fifth stage of reasoning about morality and forgiveness identified by Enright develops when the individual begins directly to reflect on the *effects* of forgiveness. Forgiveness restores social harmony and good relations – and this is a good thing as an end in itself. At this fifth stage, *I forgive because that promotes social cohesion and peace*. Few adults reach this stage, even in middle life.

More mature reflection still leads the individual to ask why social harmony matters. Gradually, moral reasoning shifts towards thinking in terms of universal principles and rights, the universal rights of all human beings to respect and justice, rights that transcend any particular society, or any particular situation. In a profound way, a commitment to respect and justice for all is a commitment to love in its purest form, free from the personal gain of being loved back, or the conditional game of controlling others through giving or withholding love. In its purest form, love gives respect and justice to all dispassionately, even-handedly, and because it is a human right. Because it is a universal right to be loved in this way, offering love is always the right thing to do. At this sixth stage, *I forgive because that is an appropriate expression of love*. Very few adults ever reach this stage. Perhaps too few of us aspire to it.[18]

Empathy and forgiveness

Many factors affect the process of forgiveness. Personality and moral development provide the broad context within which an individual is disposed to forgive – or otherwise. Aspects of the situation can also influence our tendency to forgive. It's easier to forgive a transgression in the past than one continuing in the present, or to forgive someone who is truly sorry rather than one who gloats about having hurt us, for example. Beyond all of these factors, the greatest influence on forgiveness may well be empathy.

There is an old saying, "To understand all is to forgive all." The idea here is that to understand how the situation looked from the transgressor's perspective, to understand why that person behaved as they did, creates an empathy and a compassion that foster forgiveness. And indeed, sometimes that happens, as in this story from a charity worker:

> I was giving out food parcels to needy folk. I had a list of who was to receive each parcel. Suddenly, a drug addict pushed through the queue and asked for a parcel. He wasn't on the list, and to give him anything would be to deprive someone else – all families with children. So I said no. The drug addict got very aggressive. In fact, he pulled a knife and grabbed me, holding the knife to my throat. I was terrified and angry. How dare he behave like that? In that moment, I would have stabbed him if I'd been able to. But then he said: "It's winter. I've no money, no food, nowhere to sleep. If I cut your throat, I'll be arrested and fed and safe. Why shouldn't I?" I remember thinking, "He's got a point." In that moment, all my rage toward him seeped away.[19]

Empathy can, indeed, create forgiveness – and it seems that this can create a very positive cycle: forgiveness in turn also creates empathy.[20] An attacker is often moved to a more compassionate empathy if his or her victim is forgiving, becoming less aggressive.[21] Bystanders who see the victim of some harm forgiving his or her persecutor tend to feel a positive warmth of feeling and empathy for the forgiver.[22] Newberg and his colleagues remind us that one of the great illustrations of the power of this effect comes from the fact that the early Christian Church made many converts among those who were moved by the forgiveness that Christian martyrs offered to their persecutors, in the days of the Roman Empire.[23]

Is forgiveness always healing?

The discovery of the healing power of forgiveness has led many psychotherapists and psychiatrists to give forgiveness a very prominent role in therapy. Some have gone so far as to assert that forgiveness must be at the heart of all successful healing after any traumatic experience – whether it is fate, God, someone else or ourselves that must experience forgiveness. But this stance is controversial. Like the lecturer in the story in the second chapter, many therapists reject "cheap" forgiveness, or suggest that other mechanisms for letting go of rage and revenge work just as well. Some, for example Jeanne Safer, believe that forgiveness is not always necessary or possible, and argue that there are times when we should actively refuse to forgive.[24]

Letting go of grievance: forgiveness and forgetting
The core of forgiveness, as we have defined it, involves letting go of negative feelings, thoughts or intentions towards the source of some injury or misfortune. It involves, therefore, letting go of physiological stress, letting go of brooding and moving on to a calmer and more present-focused interaction with life. There is much evidence, whether from cancer patients or victims of crime, divorcees or survivors of genocides, that "letting go" in this way has profoundly beneficial effects at many levels. Letting go of negativity is a good thing, and from this point of view, surely forgiveness is unreservedly a good thing?

Critics of forgiveness argue that there are other ways of letting go of grievance besides forgiveness. Many therapeutic and meditative practices, for example, are designed to remove negative thoughts and emotions and replace them with calm and positive ones – without any element of forgiveness being involved. The centring prayers at the end of the first chapter of this book are an example of such a practice: they are intended to refocus the mind and soul away from all distractions without yet engaging the process of forgiveness. Such practices are powerfully healing in themselves, though they need involve no element of forgiving, no sense of being forgiven – just calm.

Of course, one *can* let go of negativity without consciously thinking or meaning to forgive. This is a form of forgetting, a matter of simply putting things out of the mind – or removing one's mind from the situation. Won't that work as well as forgiveness? The answer is *no*. Forgetting and forgiving are two different things.

When we forget something, we either literally become unable to recall it, or, more commonly, we put it to the back of our mind, devaluing its importance or relevance. We may suppress it, deny, in effect, that it ever happened or that it matters. Without forgiveness, "rising above" our feelings about some bad event is very close to this sort of denial.

The trouble with denial is that it is dangerous. From a practical point of view, it is dangerous to the denier to pretend, for example, that something terrible has not happened, or that some attack never occurred. Glossing over history in this way leaves the transgressor free to offend again, or leaves us vulnerable to making the same mistake of trust or judgement again. Furthermore, forgetting is seldom complete. In the back of our minds, in some dark recess, the memory is still there, lurking, ready to re-emerge and taint our interactions with the transgressor or the world at large. Unresolved ignored fear, grievance and resentment may fester in the subconscious as Sigmund Freud was the first to realise, shaping our lives in ways we don't suspect. Simply forgetting, as the quotation from Szasz at the beginning of this chapter suggests, is naïve: it's dangerous, and nearly impossible.

Remembering is wise: it protects us from repeating the same mistakes, being attacked in the same way. But remembering alone is dangerous too: it can lead to endless rumination on the transgression, endless blame or guilt. It can create a permanent obstacle between the transgressor and his or her victim, or between the victim – or the transgressor – and the world at large, locking everyone in those roles for ever.

Forgiveness provides a way to remember, to learn from the past, but also to transcend the negative consequences of remembering. By remembering what happened and forgiving you (or myself), I engage the world as it really is, rather than as I wish it were. In forgiving, I engage you as you really are, not as we might pretend you are. But at the same time, I let go of the negativity that might otherwise harm me, let go of the destructive role of victim. In sum, forgiveness faces the truth about a situation – or oneself – honestly. Forgetting may be as useful as sticking your head in the sand. In facing and embracing the truth and *then* letting go of negativity, our understanding of life and of ourselves is stretched and enriched. In forgiving, we find a tolerance and wisdom that are absent in mere forgetting. Forgetting or even ignoring what happened may well be harmful. Forgiving provides a powerful and healthy way of transcending past hurts.

Forgiving and reconciling

Critics of forgiveness sometimes say facing the truth is all very well! Learning to accept the truth, to be tolerant and forgiving, is all very well – but there are people whom we should not forgive; there are people who simply cannot forgive. This is at the heart of many criticisms of the value of forgiveness.

For example, would it be a good thing for a child to forgive the parent who abused him or her? Is it a good thing for the survivor of a murderous attack to forgive the attacker? Many therapists would argue that it may be very harmful, if not impossible, for the victim in such situations to forgive. Wouldn't that mean that the victim would have to re-engage in a relationship with the attacker? Wouldn't the memories that would trigger, the dynamics of the interaction, do further damage?

Forgiveness is about changes in your own emotional and intentional state, your own view of the world. By our definition, it is *not* about reconciliation. This is an important point: it is possible to forgive without reconciling, and to reconcile without forgiving. Forgiveness and reconciliation are two different things. It is when these two things become confused that forgiveness may seem to be harmful.

In many situations, reconciliation is impossible. The transgressor may refuse, or be absent or even dead. Reconciliation with an aggressor may, indeed, be a dangerous and damaging thing – particularly when the victim has forgiven, but the aggressor has not changed. Simply reconciling with an abusive person may expose you to repeated abuse. It is not a healthy thing to remain in the role of victim, no matter how forgiving one feels. It is not a healthy thing to remain in a relationship that cannot be mended, even if one can forgive. Nor is it a healthy thing to be reconciled with somebody one has not forgiven: this is a recipe for disaster. Unforgiveness will keep resentment close at hand, ready to seize subtle chances for revenge, and on the lookout for further offence. There is no doubt that reconciliation is not always healing.

But there is no evidence whatever that forgiveness itself, the giving up of negative feelings and intentions towards a transgressor, is ever damaging. The evidence is overwhelming that letting go of such negativity is beneficial to physical and mental health. True forgiveness and true reconciliation might be an ideal, especially where the fractured relationships are within a family or a community. But the benefits of forgiveness, whether given or received, are real, with or without reconciliation.

Forgiveness and repentance

There is absolutely no evidence that the healing effect of forgiving is in any way affected by the remorse or repentance of the transgressor – though it is undeniably harder to forgive the unrepentant. Nor does it seem that the healing effects of being forgiven rely on having first experienced any remorse or repentance. The evidence suggests that being forgiven can have a powerful effect, whether or not one has apologised, whether or not one regrets one's actions, whether or not one feels any repentance at all. As we've seen, being forgiven tends to disarm attack: it creates empathy and warmth towards the forgiver. Being forgiven, it seems, lays the groundwork for oneself becoming repentant and forgiving.

Remorse can, in fact, be completely counterproductive as far as forgiveness or healing is concerned. Look back at the two life-stories of the woman with HIV, earlier in this chapter. The second story revolves around a crushing remorse, a terrible burden of guilt and self-blame that creates nothing but despair and hopelessness. It is the renunciation of remorse, the acceptance of the situation and of past events that creates the far more positive, far more self-forgiving first life-story. It is self-evident which is the healthier response.

Of course, repentance is not a bad thing. In fact, this emotion is the key to personal change and forgiveness, to what Christians call conversion, as we shall see in later chapters. But the evidence is that repentance can follow forgiveness as much as being the source of it. Repentance is a part of the very process of forgiveness itself.

Science, spirituality and forgiveness

Thus it seems that science and religion are in agreement: forgiveness is a very desirable thing, a healing thing. Knowing this may inspire us to try to forgive. But how can we achieve that? This is what we turn to in the next chapter.

EXERCISE

- Centre yourself, using the techniques we learned in the first chapter of this book.

- Bring yourself to bodily stillness and now ask yourself:
  How forgiving am I, as an individual? How easy do I find it to forgive myself, or others?

- Now focus again on your breathing.

- And bring yourself gently back to the world.

Reflecting on our own thoughts about forgiveness, our own past forgiveness and unforgiveness, takes us a step closer to the process of learning to forgive.

Notes

1   Stephanie Thornton, personal recollection.
2   Mark Rye et al., "Forgiveness of an Ex-spouse: How Does It Relate to Mental Health Following a Divorce?", *Journal of Divorce and Remarriage*, 41 (2004), 31-51.
3   Janette Taylor, "Moving from Surviving to Thriving: African American Women Recovering from Intimate Male Partner Abuse", *Research and Theory for Nursing Practice: An International Journal*, 18 (2004), 35-50.
4   W. Malcolm and L. Greenberg, "Forgiveness as a Process of Change in Individual Psychotherapy", in M. McCullough, K. Pargament and C. Thoresen (eds), *Forgiveness: Theory, Research and Practice* (London: Guilford Press, 2000), 179-202.
5   F. Luskin, *Forgive for Good* (San Francisco: HarperCollins, 2002), xv.
6   A. Newberg, E. d'Aquili, S. Newberg and V. deMarici, "The Neuropsychological Correlates of Forgiveness", in McCullough, Pargament and Thoresen (eds), *Forgiveness*, 91-110.
7   Luskin, *Forgive for Good*, 79.
8   Susan Nolen-Hoeksema, *Women Who Think Too Much* (London: Piatkus, 2003).
9   Richard Fitzgibbons, "Anger and the Healing Power of Forgiveness: A Psychiatrist's View", in Robert D. Enright and Joanna North (eds), *Exploring Forgiveness* (Madison: University of Wisconsin Press, 1998), 71.
10   S. Komorita, J. Hilty and C. Parks, "Reciprocity and Co-operation in Social Dilemmas", *Journal of Conflict Resolution*, 35 (1991), 494-518.
11   E. Staub et al., "Healing, Reconciliation, Forgiving and the Prevention of Violence after Genocide or Mass Killing: An Intervention and its Experimental Evaluation in Rwanda", *Journal of Social and Clinical Psychology*, 24 (2005), 297-334.
12   R. Gottlieb, "Refusing the Cure: Sophocles' Philoctetes and the Clinical Problem of Self-injurious Spite, Shame and Forgiveness", *International Journal of Psychoanalysis*, 85 (2004), 669-690.
13   R. Emmons, "Personality and Forgiveness", in McCullough, Pargament and Thoresen, *Forgiveness*, 156-174.
14   D. Rowe, "Genetics, Temperament and Personality", in R. Hogan, J. Johnson and S. Briggs (eds), *Handbook of Personality Psychology* (San Diego: Academic Press, 1997), 367-386.

15   Emmons, "Personality and Forgiveness", in McCullough, Pargament and Thoresen, *Forgiveness*, 156-174.

16   L. Temoshok and P. Chandra, "The Meaning of Forgiveness in a Specific Cultural Context", in McCullough, Pargament and Thoresen, *Forgiveness*, 41-64.

17   R. Enright, "The Moral Development of Forgiveness", in W. Kurtines and J. Gewirtz (eds), *Handbook of Moral Development and Behaviour*, 3 vols, i (New Jersey: L. Erlbaum, 1991), 123-152; R. Enright, E. Gassin and C. Wu, "Forgiveness: A Developmental View", *Journal of Moral Education*, 21 (1992), 99-114.

18   Enright, Gassin and Wu.

19   Correspondence to the authors.

20   Newberg, et al., "Neuropsychological", 91-111.

21   R. Enright, "Counselling within the Forgiveness Triad: On Forgiving, Receiving Forgiveness and Self-forgiveness", *Counselling and Values*, 40 (1996), 107-126.

22   S. Kanekar and S. Merchant, "Aggression, Retaliation and Religious Affiliation", *Journal of Social Psychology*, 117 (1982), 295-296.

23   Newberg, et al., "Neuropsychological".

24   See Jeanne Safer, *Forgiving and Not Forgiving: A New Approach to Resolving Intimate Betrayal* (New York: Avon Books, 1999).

5

The process of forgiveness

"All you need is love."
John Lennon

Recently, I was talking to a friend about forgiveness. We agreed that forgiveness is good for us. But! "It's all very well wanting to forgive," he said, "but how on earth does one go about doing it?"

Accepting different paths to forgiveness

For some, forgiveness comes almost instantly. So it was for Michael, whose story was told in chapter one, and Marie, whose story was told in chapter three. Both had their sons murdered. Both felt all the grief and injustice of the situation. But both were able to transcend the moment, to relinquish all idea of vengeance and hate, to forgive and channel their energy into compassion. In each case, life was given new meaning, new peace through the power of this forgiveness.

Living forgiveness

There are some individuals for whom such forgiveness is as natural as breathing. It is their automatic reaction, a reaction they characteristically bring to every situation. Such individuals are very few and far between, and very special. They daily live out a spirituality that shines from them and awes us all. There's no telling where we may find these rare spirits: at the head of religions that preach forgiveness – in the Vatican, in mosques and temples, the redoubts of the Dalai Lama? Perhaps in our neighbours, or the people we pass anonymously in the street? Or even in an unemployed carpenter? Are these rare souls born with this spiritual strength of forgiveness, or must they develop it, deliberately embrace it? Every great world religion believes that each one of us is *capable* of becoming transcendentally forgiving, and that we are called to do so. To discover, or develop within ourselves the constant power of forgiveness is a virtue. Could we all achieve it?

Psychology finds differences between one individual and another in the extent to which we understand forgiveness, or can forgive, or even want to try. Such differences change with age and experience, reflecting changes in the values and beliefs and insight that imbue the individual. These changes can occur in the flash of an eye – or take many years of hard work and effort. For the Christian, there is help at hand in this great venture, if only we open our hearts to the Holy Spirit. Other religions use other words to point to the same truth. Science and religion combine to suggest that it is possible that we can, one day, with enough commitment, find the capacity for a flowing transcendental forgiveness in ourselves. *But how?*

Shocked into forgiveness

Sometimes, a truly awful experience can act as a powerful "wake-up" call in our spiritual lives. Something so terrible, so apparently unbearable, happens that we can no longer be the person we were, nor live the life we were living. All the meaning is taken from our lives, all that we have loved, all the goals we have worked for, all the purposes that shaped our actions are gone, and gone for ever.

In such a moment there is the possibility of utter despair, of crumbling to nothing, of giving up all hope – of refusing even life itself. The temptation to surrender to such total defeat can be strong. Why bother, when all is pain and hopelessness, when all I've tried so hard to do has failed, been made pointless, when there seems no way out? Those who work with the suicidal recognise this state of being, and respect it. This is the "rock bottom" of the human soul: a searing, unendurable pain – or an equally unendurable dull and endless emptiness. No one gives up on life lightly. Nor should we despise those who touch rock bottom. Rather, we should embrace them in our love. To despair and surrender is not the only possibility.

The human spirit is astonishingly resilient. Faced with an assault on the very heart of our existence, there is also the possibility of raging against fate or against the author of our misfortune. In many ways, this is the response of the survivor, a rejection of what has happened, a refusal to accept defeat, a commitment to fighting back. But fighting back in this way carries its own penalties. We may allow ourselves to be consumed by grief, resentment, a sense of injustice, and lead lives of bitterness. We may be consumed by the desire for vengeance, leading lives of hate. Many take these paths. Few enjoy them.

There is also the possibility of being spun into a new reality, into a world marked by a pragmatic acceptance of what has happened, and by a healing forgiveness that transforms the pain and creates new meanings and purposes. Somehow, from suffering and despair comes a new conception of the human condition, a new and transcendental conception of our own personal lives and significance, and a new spiritual strength – a new peace and joy.

Religion has long understood the potential for despair and suffering to yield such transformations in the soul. Science is now discovering the same thing: terrible loss, or the realisation of one's own impending death through illness or disaster, or even the recognition that we have narrowly escaped such a thing, can potentially change what seems important to us, casting our values in a new light. It can transport us into a peace and joy that is beyond the comprehension of those leading ordinary, unchallenged lives.

What makes one individual respond to pain and disaster with despair or hate, and another respond with forgiving love and healing peace? The longing for the spiritual grace to forgive is there whenever we hear the plea: don't let this death, this mutilation, be for nothing! Don't let it fuel more! Let something good grow from it!

One can only be awed and moved by how many of the bereaved, the suffering, endorse these views. But living out such forgiveness is hard. The desire for healing, for forgiveness, is not always enough.

Struggling to forgive

For many of us, much of the time, forgiveness is not instant. We are not saints who, either through extraordinary grace or through long years of working to develop the virtue of forgiveness, have become inherently, all-consumingly and automatically forgiving. And – if we have been fortunate – we have not personally had to face any event so fundamentally challenging as to be capable of resetting our spiritual lives in one moment of transforming insight. For most of us, forgiveness can be a long, hard slog; perhaps even life's work.

Virtue is a facility in doing good. For the person who has developed the virtue of forgiveness, forgiveness comes naturally, for all its challenges. But the difficulty in taking that first step towards virtue can be hard! And our inability to forgive can be extremely painful. A woman writes:

> I have been estranged from my best friend for ten years. I supported her through her divorce, both emotionally through regular phone calls and by providing practical support. I liaised between her and her ex-husband as she asked me to. I offered no judgements. When my own marriage crumbled a few years later, things were very different. My soon-to-be ex-husband visited her to deliver Christmas gifts from me, which I had sent via my child who was on an "access" weekend. He phoned to tell me that he would not do such a thing again, because my friend was gloating over our situation.

> I have never, in all these years, had a single expression of sympathy from her over the breakdown of my marriage, nor any gesture of emotional or practical support. Far from it: she attacked me when I was down. Her incomprehensible aggression towards me has shocked our friends.

> Our estrangement hurts deeply: a pain I hate. And, it runs counter to my Christian commitment: for a number of years, I could not

pray the Lord's Prayer. My voice would falter as I came to the phrase, "forgive us our trespasses as we forgive those who trespass against us". I was so hurt that I could not forgive her. Because of that, I felt that God could not forgive me for the very many things for which I needed forgiveness. Reconciliation seemed, and still seems impossible. So I have lost a friend, and am unable to live up to my spiritual call, and am wretched.[1]

Wanting to forgive and being unable to do so can be a very painful experience. It can be damaging, too, especially when the one I cannot forgive is myself. Am I a lesser being because forgiveness is a hard struggle for me, because I am not instantly transported to grace, as others may be?

The hardest step in any journey, and certainly in the journey to forgiveness, is the very first step: *wanting* to forgive. No one who has taken that great step need be ashamed, even if the fruit of forgiveness is not instantly in reach. In fact, grace begins with our desire to reject unforgiveness, our desire to forgive. As soon as we set out to do that each step we take along the way, however small or difficult it seems, develops that grace within us, moving us towards forgiveness. And as we slowly become open to forgiveness we may find it, not just for the one particular event, but for many things. Our outlook changes, and, however imperceptible it may seem, the virtue of forgiveness grows within us.

For most of us, forgiveness is very hard. We'd so very much like to do it! But we can't. Part of the problem is that we misunderstand what is involved: we think forgiveness requires reconciliation, for example, when it need not. Or we think it means denying that there is a problem, or letting go of anger, when it does not. It is right to be angry when people behave badly, and wrong to pretend that their behaviour is acceptable. We fear forgiveness will mean that we must put ourselves in the way of further attack, or further pain, when it does not mean that at all. The woman described above suffered all these confusions. Spiritual guidance allowed her to see that forgiveness required only letting go of her resentment and grievance against her friend, letting go of any desire to hurt in return.

But part of the problem of forgiveness is that we simply don't know how to do it. I may want to forgive, may be desperate, in fact, to find a way to let go of my pain and grievance and to heal wounds, but may have no idea how to do that, no idea what practical steps to take, nor how to interpret my experiences along the way. And that is what the rest of this chapter is about.

The natural process of forgiveness

Eventually, most people (but not all) get over a grievance, let go of resentment, lose interest in revenge and move on in their lives. There is a natural rhythm to this process, a natural progression that tends to go in stages. Different writers give different names to these stages, but the underlying sequence is more or less the same.[2]

These stages take time. Time heals, doesn't it? But the truth is that it is not the passive passage of time that heals, but the powerful and dynamic process of forgiveness. Without engaging that process of forgiveness, moving forward through it, time may trap us in one stage or another, denying us the possibility of true healing.

Stage one – Denial

Something terrible happens, and at first we cannot accept that this is true: *this can't be happening to me!* Our minds refuse to face reality, refuse to face the shock or pain. Many people faced with personal trauma say: at first, I refused to believe it. I pretended it was not happening! I told no one, as if telling someone else would make it real, make it true. As if saying nothing, behaving as if it were not true, would mean that it were not true.

Such denial is a powerful psychological mechanism to protect us from the unbearable, what Sigmund Freud called a "defence mechanism". It is as if the mind goes into shock, goes into a world where the unbearable has not happened and need not be dealt with: *it didn't happen, or maybe it doesn't matter!* But this is a surreal world, an untrue world that does not honour our real needs, our real feelings. It produces strange, shocked behaviour and disconnected feelings. By its very nature, denial separates us from reality. It prevents us from looking honestly at how we feel and what we fear. It cannot heal us in the real world, therefore, and it cannot easily last. Maintaining such denial is a costly business.

Let's take the example of Jane. Five years after being cruelly ridiculed and rejected by her lover, Jane maintains that she is now completely over the hurt - but that she will never trust another man again. She doesn't connect her lack of trust with her unhealed hurt. To examine that connection might be too frightening! As Sidney and Suzanne Simon write: "You may be afraid because once you admit how you were hurt and, even more so, what you have done because of the hurt, you will have to change. You will have to act and react differently from the way you have in the past, and you do not know how to do that. You do not know whether or not you could survive if you did that."[3]

Sidney and Suzanne Simon believe that everyone who has been hurt spends some time in this first stage of denial, and some can remain stuck in this stage for many years. Such denial is expressed by shrugging off past hurts as if they did not matter, did not need addressing, were somehow now irrelevant, consigned to the past, or were merely mundane and normal. Emotional hurt cannot be healed in these ways, any more than the effects of a truck plunging through a bus queue of children could be "healed" by pretending that the resulting death and destruction somehow do not matter, need not be addressed, are irrelevant, happened five years ago and are therefore now somehow "history", "water under the bridge", or that such horrible events are normal.

Denial cannot heal. In fact, to deny that we are hurt, or that there is a problem, denies our wounds the respect they deserve, and denies us all possibility of acknowledging and addressing those wounds. To pretend it is either not happening or doesn't matter is to commit to living in ruins and debris.

No amount of time spent in denial can ever heal. It is not time that heals, but the more active process of moving towards forgiveness. To move forward, to move towards forgiveness, to handle the problem, we must first consciously accept what has happened, and consciously accept that we are wounded. And in a profound way, while accepting what has happened, we have to assert our own value: we have to assert that we are not just physically or emotionally wounded, but existentially wounded. We have to be clear in our own minds that what has happened does not meet our ideas of what is "right" or "fair" – and that we are resentful, regretful about it.

Stage two – Self-blame
Strangely, the first step out of denial, the first reaction of those who admit they have been hurt, is very often to blame themselves for whatever has happened. What kind of person would suffer some misfortune and then blame themselves? The answer seems to be – almost all of us.

If only I had been a more loveable child, a better child, daddy would have loved me, he wouldn't have hit me! If only I had been a better wife, my husband would not have broken his vows and had affairs, would not have run off with other women. If I'd been a better employee/had chosen a different route to the shops/had not fallen in love, I would not have been sacked/trapped in the wreckage of a car crash/had my heart broken ...

If only. If only I had behaved differently, thought differently, felt differently, I would not be in this mess now. Who has never had such a thought? Why do we blame ourselves this way? Why do we move from denial straight on to punishing ourselves for whatever has happened?

How terrifying it is, to contemplate a world in which our fate is random, unpredictable, entirely out of our control! How could one feel confidence, or plan, or hope or dream in such a world? The human mind recoils from the prospect. We want, so very much, to feel that life is, at least to some degree, at least when it really matters, in our control! It's comforting, then, to assume that that is so: that whatever has befallen us could have been avoided, had we acted differently. If it were somehow our own fault, we could learn to avoid that mistake in the future, learn to avoid further pain. And so we prefer to blame ourselves, rather than facing the fact that human life is unpredictable, uncertain, and ultimately beyond our control.

This stage of self-blame is a healing step beyond denial because it acknowledges the reality of what has befallen us. It reasserts our right to determine our lives – or at least, our response to what happens in our lives. Even taking responsibility for the wrong things is a healthier response than pretending that we are unhurt!

But self-blame is as much of a trap as denial. By blaming myself for what happened I add to the pain of the original assault by repeatedly punishing myself for it. Self-blame rubs salt in our wounds. It cannot possibly ever heal, any more than denial can, for it rests on a subtler, more invidious form of denial: it rests on denial of the very nature of the human condition, of what it means to be human; it rests on denial of the fragility and vulnerability, the ultimately uncontrollable nature of our lives. Until we accept these things, we cannot begin to address them any more than we can address a pain we do not acknowledge to exist.

Stage three – Victimhood
Of course, if it is not my fault that I am wounded, then I am the hapless victim of events, or of some malign abuser.

Recognition that one is a victim is a major step forward through the process of recovery from some assault or misfortune. It acknowledges that some wound has been suffered, and that this wound was out of the victim's control: it was ordained by someone else, or by malign circumstances. Now, the wounded person has, for the first time, conceptualised the heart of the problem: I am wounded, and I am vulnerable, in a world that can be malign and pitiless, and I must come to terms with these frightening things.

There is a natural sympathy for the victims of trauma, of whatever origin. We who observe such victims may be powerfully moved to pity. Victims themselves may be powerfully moved to self-pity. In perspective, this is no bad thing: to move from the self-punishment of assuming blame for one's wounds, and to offer oneself the compassion one would offer someone else similarly afflicted is a greatly healing thing.

But negotiating and surviving the stage of victimhood takes subtle judgement and understanding. Recognising that one is wounded, and that this is not one's own fault, that what has happened is unfair, unjust, completely outside one's control and against one's will, is a healthy perception, starkly defining what has happened and what one must come to terms with. But it's easy to slip from here into the assumption that one's wounds and vulnerability are so outrageous as to be unique – uniquely unfair or outrageous – and so to dwell on one's status as a victim needing special consideration, Making *this* the centre of one's life, one's world view, one's conversations, is profoundly misguided, and profoundly unhealthy. It denies the greater reality, which is that *all* human lives are fragile, vulnerable and outside individual control. It denies the possibility that everyone deserves the compassion and succour that our own victimhood demands. It misses the real point, which is that our own pain and vulnerability are but one aspect of the human condition as a whole.

To wallow in one's own victimhood may be comforting at some level. But it cannot bring true healing. It steers us away from the real issues of acceptance, forgiveness and spiritual transcendence every bit as much as denial and self-blame, because it steers us away from truth.

Stage four – Indignation
Of course, a core element of the recognition that one is the victim of an injustice is the perception that someone or something did this to me! How dare they! Why should they get away with it? Sooner or later, this perception is likely to assert itself – and it is good that it does!

Now it is not merely the victim's perception that what one has suffered is unfair or wrong that dominates. There is also the idea that anger against the transgressor may be right – and that revenge, or at least retribution, may be in order.

Anger is a healthy response to abuse. It energises us for action, for fresh interaction with the world where denial, self-blame and victimhood encourage passivity and acquiescence. It is the motivating force that says – as we should – stand up for yourself! Stand up for what is right! Don't let injustice, wrong or evildoers get away with it!

But anger is a problem for very many of us, and particularly for those of us who seek God. We tend to believe that anger is necessarily and always bad, always a window for sin. Should we not, always, "turn the other cheek"? Should we not always suppress our anger, "seventy-seven times"?

Indeed, anger can be bad! If my anger fuels only a desire to hurt those who have hurt me, fuels only a commitment to vengeance, then it is likely to be a route to destruction and self-destruction. The responses of hatred and vengeance can have no positive outcome, either for ourselves or for those we attack. They are always wrong. But anger is not hate, and it is not vengeance. It is just anger: the emotion that focuses on and rejects what is wrong, unfair, unjust. Never to feel anger would mean never recognising or accepting the wrongness of human exploitation, of torture, of abuse. Should Jews today feel no anger about Hitler's holocaust? Should I, on holiday in Amsterdam, standing in the building where Anne Frank and her family hid and from which she was dragged to her death in a concentration camp, have felt no anger, no *wrongness* in those events? Should I read of acts of torture, genocidal murders, cynical executions today and feel no outrage, no anger?

To reject anger is to reject all forms of judgement. Perhaps it is wrong, to look into the eyes of a torturer, a serial killer, and say, you are evil and I will suppress you. But how can it be wrong to look at the actions of the torturer, the actions of the serial killer, and say, those actions are evil, and I will suppress them?

Anger that fuels vengeance is bad. Anger directed at injustice is good. It is drawing the line between these things that poses the problem. To become angry about injustice is a healing, healthful thing! It marks the return of an appropriate judgement, an appropriate commitment to endorse what is good and reject what is bad. But to become consumed with anger, to refuse to put it in perspective, or never to let it go is destructive. This is the route to endless rage, to vengeance, hatred. In a world where we see anger as the focus, as the legitimate core, we may move beyond an angry response to this or that and become, ourselves, anger personified: we may become aggressive, angry people, polluting new situations, new relationships, with this anger. This cannot heal our wounds! Rather, it is likely to create new ones, as our anger alienates those around us, causing new rifts, new attacks and new wounds.

Stage five – Surviving
The stages of denial, self-blame, victimhood and indignation – righteous anger – are natural responses to assaults. But each, in its own way, locks us in the hurt, for ever focused on that hurt as the defining

event of life, endlessly reacting to it. None of these reactions move on from the assault. Rather, each and every one is determined and driven by what has happened. There is no escape, no new perspective on the event, no assertion of higher values. Each stage looks back to what has happened, and defines itself in terms of that.

It is when we begin to move beyond the hurts of the past, becoming determined to engage life in ways that are not defined or driven by those hurts, that we start to become true survivors. Only when the past and its hurts, no longer dominate do we begin to escape from those hurts, begin to be able to engage the world afresh and find new purpose and meaning, new hope and joy within it.

As Sidney and Suzanne Simon put it: "In the survivor stage you spend more and more time looking ahead towards health instead of back towards your pain."[4] You begin to realise that despite everything that happened to you, you are still alive, still in charge of your own life, and now want to get your life back under your own control. You recognise that living in denial, self-blame, victimhood or indignation is not healthy. The hurts and wounds of the past were real, but they belong to the past. You don't have to bring them into the future. The survivor draws a line in the sand and proclaims that the resentments, grudges, bitterness and unforgiveness will not pass this line. They will not be part of the future which is opening up. "Although you may have thought this before, in the survivor stage you actually do it. After years of merely responding to the people and circumstances that you happened to encounter, you take back the reins that you handed over to fate and play an active role in determining your own destiny. You become an actor instead of a reactor, a player in the game of life rather than a spectator watching from the sidelines while life passes you by."[5]

Surviving means much more than a grim hanging on. It means a determination to let go of the past, to accept that it is gone. We have to accept that in its entirety: we have lost something good, but the moment of loss is gone too. We are here, in this new world, and must engage it for what it is – and for what it can be. We must let go of the past and move on, embracing the present. This is the response of health – an honest realism that courageously re-embraces life.

Stage six – Reintegration
It's a mistake to think that we progress steadily through the five stages of recovery we have described here, one after another, ticking each one off as we pass through it and leaving each behind as we move forward. In reality, we may slide backwards and forwards between one and another, or experience more than one at the same time: even a commitment to surviving may be punctuated by a resurgence of anger, self-pity, self-blame or denial. It is in reaching towards each next stage that we begin to recover, begin to move towards a healing forgiveness. It is in shifting the balance of our focus from denial towards survival that we lay the foundations for this true healing.

But in its own way, the "survivor" stage takes us right back to the beginning of the healing cycle. We have put our reactions to the past behind us. We refuse to focus on or be defined by that past. We will address the present! We will wipe the slate clean, start again, become new people, in this new world we now inhabit. All of this is very healthy – but it is also a new and more subtle form of denial. For the truth is that we are *not* newborn people, starting with a fresh slate. We are the products of all that we have experienced, all that we have felt and suffered, all that we have done and had done to us. There is no way to avoid this fundamental truth. At the survivor stage, we begin to engage new things, but we have not yet integrated our new selves with our past, and that is why that past can break through and drag us back into denial, or anger, or victimhood or self-blame.

Complete healing requires complete integration of all that we are, all that we have been. Unless we can integrate our entire experience into a coherent whole and be happy with it, the past and our old reactions to it will always hover somewhere, always have the potential to attack and undermine us. To heal fully we must accept ourselves and our whole history completely and unconditionally.

How is it possible to integrate all that has happened to us, good and bad, into one coherent whole, to accept that whole for what it is, to be at peace with it? The truth is that every little event that befalls us, every hurt we suffer, every mistake we make, every triumph we experience shapes us – and every one of these things enriches us. It is through setbacks that we develop courage and perseverance, through pain that we grow in insight and understanding and in our capacity for compassion. We develop more richly as people through suffering and setbacks than through sunshine and success. And however hard it may be to come to this realisation and integration, achieving it is vital if we are to reach true peace and forgiveness.

An unhappy love affair can score the heart deeply, creating wounds and loss that seem impossible to heal. Does one ever recover? If "recover" means returning to the person one was before the affair, as if the affair and all its hurts never existed, then the answer is no. Nor would it be healthy to do that, even if one could! The hypnotherapist Paul McKenna is often asked to hypnotise the broken-hearted to remove all their memories of the lost lover, and all their feelings of pain and anger. He refuses. Such hypnotherapy would be the ultimate in denial! Yes, it would allow the recipient to "survive", to engage the world without bitterness, pain, hate, despair. But it would remove all chance of that person growing from the experience, learning from what had happened.

It is through the experiences of living, of loving, of failing and being failed that we come to understand ourselves, our fellow human beings, our place in the universe. We cannot have all that we want! In fact, we will probably suffer quite a lot of setbacks – some trivial, some serious – in life. The only way to avoid pain is to avoid life. The unlived life is sterile, arid, barren – and pointless: more pointless than the life re-routed by events but still engaging and learning from the experience of living.

Does one ever recover from the heartbreak of a failed love affair? Not by pretending it doesn't matter. Not through the absurdity of taking all the blame, nor assigning all the blame to the other. Not by trying to live as if it never existed. One recovers by coming to realise that this experience, for all its hurts, has given one gifts that could never have been acquired in any other way. There are the gifts from the good moments, which are easy to recognise. But there are also the more subtle gifts of the bad moments: the harder lessons. It is through integrating all of these lessons, through incorporating them into who and what we are, that we develop, that we become fully ourselves.

In accepting that we are the product of all that has happened, and that we have been enriched by it, we lay the true foundations for forgiveness. As Rowan Williams, the Archbishop of Canterbury, puts it: "If forgiveness is liberation, it is also a recovery of the past in hope, a return of the memory, in which what is potentially threatening, destructive, despair-inducing, in the past is transfigured into a ground of hope."[6] As I accept my past, and everything that has happened to me in the past, I can accept myself just as I am in the present in a new and healing way. In accepting myself unconditionally in the present I can also accept the hurts of the past that contributed in their own way to who I am in the present. In accepting *all* that I am, I become more fully and honestly myself.

Forgiveness must happen within us before we can offer it to other people. Before we can forgive, we must reach a complete acceptance of ourselves, our history, all that we have experienced and all that we are. This acceptance is, in truth, what forgiveness is. In reaching such acceptance we will inevitably reconstrue the role others have played in making us who we are. Pain wakes us up! It gives us the opportunity to learn. The writer Barbara De Angelis suggests that we can choose to view those who have caused us pain, those who have challenged us to "wake up", as *teachers* rather than enemies.[7] Without their intervention, I would not have faced this challenge, would not have had the opportunity to learn this lesson, or to grow in empathy and compassion, insight and understanding. Such a grateful perception – coupled with the perception that these "teachers" too are fallible, suffering human beings – allows us to offer them the unconditional acceptance and forgiveness we have discovered for ourselves.

Stage seven – Forgiveness
As we move through the active re-engagement with the world that characterises the survivor stage, and then the reflective insight that characterises reintegration, something extraordinary begins to happen. Softly, subtly, without really noticing, we move towards the miracle of true forgiveness. One day we wake up and realise the pain, the rage, the resentment are not there. We have forgiven!

In a letter to his friend Malcolm, C. S. Lewis described how this realisation can catch us by surprise: "Last week while at prayer, I suddenly discovered – or felt as if I did – that I had forgiven someone I had been trying to forgive for over thirty years."[8]

How to speed the process of forgiveness?
Forgiveness cannot be commanded as a mere act of the will. Who could command the heart to heal, the soul to enlarge, by issuing an order? Could I become twice as good a golfer or twice as slender simply by commanding it?

Where golfing or slimming are concerned, the idea that we could achieve our goal simply by wishing it were so is laughable. Childish! Absurd. But in the matter of forgiveness, our efforts are often as childish and as absurd as that. We wish we could forgive and then are surprised or self-critical when it doesn't happen. To play better golf we must learn new techniques and we must practise; to slim we must change our diet, do more exercise. Like golf or slimming, forgiveness takes work.

As we have seen throughout this book, forgiveness is a fight on two fronts: the fight to let go of the pain we have suffered, the damage to our self-esteem and our sense of our own value that this assault has caused, and our fight to let go of the outrage and feelings of vengeance towards those who have inflicted this damage upon us. To overcome the first we need healing. To overcome the second, we need to grow in humanity and in spirituality.

Harnessing the natural processes of forgiveness

Bit by bit the natural processes of forgiveness we have described bring us healing and enlarge our souls. But not everyone passes through all these stages: many become trapped at some stage or other and never receive the blessing of forgiveness. It's easy to believe that how I feel today, whether that be denial or self-blame or indignation, is the right response or the only one I can have, and so to fix myself in that state until some outside event jolts me out of it. It needn't be like that. Through understanding the natural stages of forgiveness we gain insight. We come to understand how the feeling we have today fits into a broader picture – and how that feeling can change, as the process of forgiveness unfolds. We can harness that insight, using it deliberately and consciously to engage in the process of forgiveness, deliberately and consciously working through each stage and moving on to the next.

Most of us, when faced with some situation that challenges us to forgive, spend many years or even become trapped in the early stages of the process. We become trapped in the pain of denial, self-blame, self-pity, or outrage. Pretending it is not so is pointless. Such feelings need to be expressed and acknowledged, given the respect they deserve. And that is the first step we can take in speeding up the natural rhythms of forgiveness: we can give ourselves permission to feel all of those things, we can explore those feelings, reflect on them, accept them, even embrace them. We can, in other words, deliberately and consciously plunge into the areas that need to be addressed, rather than wait for events to carry us there. We can commit ourselves to work through these things, rather than waiting passively for it to happen somehow.

While we are trapped in pain, the early stages of forgiveness, the later stages of survival and integration can seem unimaginable. We literally can't imagine how our lives could be healed or how we can accept what has happened, let go of it and move on. Simply knowing what the stages of survival and integration will be like can bring comfort – and can show us what to work for. The idea that even terrible experiences shape who we are and enrich us – that our enemies may be teachers to whom one day we will be grateful for the painful lessons taught – this may seem absurd, impossible. But by deliberately and consciously considering the possibility that this is true, we put ourselves in the right place to speed our path to a full integration of our experience and a true and healing forgiveness. By knowing where we are going we travel more swiftly along the path, working for forgiveness in a focused way rather than merely willing it or waiting passively for it to happen.

Harnessing spiritual resources for forgiveness

Forgiveness is a human process, drawing on the resources of our minds to create a growing awareness and acceptance of the realities of our situation and the human condition. Growing insight creates change in how we feel towards ourselves and others, a letting go of despair, rage, hate and an embracing of hope, peace – and love. For in forgiving, we come to love our own lives again. In forgiving, we offer acceptance to those who have harmed us, an awareness of and respect for their humanity. This is a harder form of love: it is love for its own sake. Such love offered to an enemy is the highest expression of forgiveness, the highest expression of love.

It is this connection of forgiveness and love that reveals the fact that forgiving is, intrinsically, a spiritual process. In forgiving we raise our sights beyond the particulars of our human characteristics and experiences. In effect, we say: my attacker's human character has terrible flaws, and his or her actions are evil. Nonetheless, he or she has a value that transcends those things, and in forgiving I show respect for that value. Of course, that transcendental value is spiritual value.

In forgiving, then, we are orienting to the spiritual value that lies within human character and experience. Understanding this opens up a new and powerful route to forgiveness, just as insight into the psychological processes of forgiveness provides a map to speed our way. We can, if we choose, embrace the spiritual dimension of forgiveness from the outset, and use it to speed our way to achieving full forgiveness.

No matter how wounded or damaged our lives may be, there is healing comfort in recognising the profound truth that we have a spiritual essence, a true self whose value, meaning and potential soar beyond the present circumstances. However damaged our lives may be, we are precious: precious in God's eyes. Truly feeling this divine love puts the darkest of our feelings of self-blame and self-pity in perspective. In God's eyes, we are whole and perfect.

Furthermore, whatever those who have harmed us have done, they too have a value and meaning that transcend their behaviour. They too are precious in God's eyes. As hard as it can be to accept this when we are wounded, it is the truth. Recognising our shared spiritual value may help us to lay aside vengeance and hate. Orienting to our enemies on a spiritual plane rather than just on the level of the hurt or the enmity changes everything.

Focusing on our spiritual selves, the selves that transcend our human characteristics and experience, can also speed the way to a reintegration of our lives. From the perspective of our spiritual value it may be easier to lay aside denial of what has happened in our human experience, to "stand back" as it were and look for the broader pattern of meaning in our lives.

All through this process, God reaches out a hand to help us. God is there with us in our pain, and there offering us a way forward. It is God's love for us that creates our spiritual value. God's love for us will heal our hurts, if we let it in. It can offer a new dimension in which to relate to our enemies, to offer them love instead of hate. And it offers us a new perspective, a "higher ground" from which to seek reintegration in our lives. Freely flowing through us, love can speed our path to healing and forgiveness. And, in fact, to forgive, all we need is love.

EXERCISE
- Centre yourself, using the techniques we learned in the first chapter of this book.

- Bring yourself to bodily stillness and reflect on the first four stages of healing: denial, self-blame, victimhood, indignation. What role are these things playing in your life? Focus on recognising how these things may be affecting you, without judging yourself.

- Are you ready to step beyond these things and towards survival? Are you ready to take the even greater leap towards self-acceptance, integration and forgiveness?

- Accept yourself, your situation, just as it is. Look again at what has hurt you, at the setbacks you've suffered. What can they teach you? How can they enrich you?

- Now focus again on your breathing.

- And bring yourself gently back to the world.

The desire to forgive is only the beginning. To achieve forgiveness, we must embrace all the hurt we have suffered, all the feelings that hurt has provoked. And we must go beyond this to discover what good has come from all this, what good could come from all this. At the heart of forgiveness is acceptance: of what has been, of what now is, and of what can be.

Notes

1   Correspondence to the authors.

2   Sidney B. Simon and Suzanne Simon, *Forgiveness: How to Make Peace with your Past and Get on with your Life* (New York: Warner Books, 1990), 77-240; William Meninger, *The Process of Forgiveness* (New York: Continuum, 1996), 47-72; Beverly Flanigan, *Forgiving the Unforgiveable* (New York: Macmillan, 1992), 71-186. In the present chapter we have followed the stages outlined by Simon and Simon.

3   Simon and Simon, *Forgiveness*, 80.

4   Ibid. 182.

5   Ibid.

6   Cited in Gregory Jones, *Embodying Forgiveness: A Theological Analysis* (Grand Rapids, MI: W. B. Eerdmans, 1995), 177.

7   Barbara De Angelis, *Secrets about Life Every Woman Should Know: Ten Principles for Spiritual and Emotional Fulfilment* (London: Thorsons, 2000).

8   Cited in Jones, *Embodying Forgiveness*, 236.

6

Accepting the gift of forgiveness

"Father, forgive me, for I have sinned."
Traditional Catholic prayer of confession

If it is hard to forgive others for what they have done to us, it can be even harder to feel forgiven for what we ourselves have done – or failed to do. In fact, for many of us, the greatest challenge posed by forgiveness is that of accepting that we are forgiven.

Facing the need for forgiveness
We are not always aware of our own need for forgiveness. Often, we are simply unaware of the effects of our words or actions – not realising, for example, that a piece of casual gossip can lead to serious wounds in someone else's life, or that a careless action causes difficulties for others.

St Philip Neri, a famous confessor in Rome in the sixteenth century, taught a society lady a very good lesson about her gossiping. When she confessed to the saint that she "had engaged in a little bit of gossip" he gave her this penance. The lady was to fill a large bag with the feathers of a goose and go up to the top of the Janiculum hill on a very windy day, throw the feathers into the wind and then come back and see him. Having carried out her unusual penance, she returned to the saint to report her success. What a shock she got when he told her that the second part of her penance was to collect all the feathers again. "But", she exclaimed, "the feathers are all over Rome." The saint responded, "And so is your gossip."

Often we act from the best of intentions but get things wrong: we are insensitive to another person's perspective or needs and, without meaning to, we cause a hurt and damage that we fail to recognise. Surprisingly often this kind of insensitivity is at the root of even criminal behaviours, which is why empathy training turns some criminals away from crime. Or we may be deliberately wounding to someone else and feel justified in that aggression, believing it to be our right, given what they have done to us, and overlooking how far short of our own values our behaviour is falling. We may find it so difficult to face our own bad behaviour that we twist it around in our minds, so that our guilt turns to self-righteous resentment against those we have harmed, "justifying" what we have done.

All of these problems in recognising our own need for forgiveness stem from the limitations in our human awareness. We don't realise what we've done. Sometimes we never come to realise it. Other times, the full shame of some action eventually comes to us very much later, as in the case of Martin:

> I was a real go-getter. I was determined to get to the top of my firm, be the boss. I knew I had what it takes to do that. And I was successful, I made it to the top. I ran a tight ship, kept the business on the rails, made tough decisions when they were needed. At the time I was proud of myself. Only later, after I had retired, did I start to look back and regret things, like putting the profits of the business first, even when that meant causing real hardship to people. I wish I'd been more humane in the way I treated people, wish I'd treated them more like people and less like tools. I wish I could go back and apologise and make things right. Sometimes I cringe when I remember certain things that happened, certain things I did. But at the time, everyone praised me, and I saw nothing wrong with what I was doing at all.[1]

Few of us commit very grave sins in this life; but many of us do things that we later greatly regret. Awareness of our need for forgiveness comes in small steps, as our insight and understanding mature. We blame ourselves for the mistakes we made out of ignorance or immaturity, the things we did in spite or anger, the targets we set ourselves and missed, the values we betrayed, and we are abject in our hunger for forgiveness. How could anyone ever forgive me? How could I ever forgive myself?

The pain of unforgiveness
This growing insight into our own need for forgiveness can be extremely painful. Often, awareness comes too late: the people from whom we need that forgiveness are not there to give it. The parent we hurt by our selfishness as a young adult is long dead by the time we become aware of that selfishness; the child we bullied, the person we wronged or failed to help, has long vanished from our lives. Even when we can contact those from whom we seek forgiveness, we may not always be offered it. A partner may harbour too much bitterness after a divorce ever to offer forgiveness, however much we ask for it; a colleague may refuse to forgive us for slights or rivalries. Forgiveness may simply not be forthcoming from those we have wounded, those from whom we most need it.

And yet, our need for forgiveness is very strong. Without it we are ill at ease in the world, ill at ease with ourselves – perhaps even filled with self-loathing and self-rejection. What comfort can there be for us?

Finding comfort through forgiveness
What right do I have to feel forgiven, if those I have harmed have been unwilling or unable to forgive me, if I have not asked for forgiveness before it is too late? Christ's answer is that, just as *giving* forgiveness is my inalienable right, no matter whether my attacker is repentant, no matter whether reconciliation is possible, no matter whether I have received restitution or not, so it is my inalienable right to receive forgiveness – no matter whether my victim is willing or able to receive restitution or to accept reconciliation. All I need do, to receive forgiveness, is to repent and open my heart to the healing gift of forgiveness.

Christ's message is clear: *all* sins can be forgiven. Through Christ, it is our right to be forgiven. If we look for forgiveness through Christ, we will find it, whether those we have offended forgive us or not. Through Christ, we are assured of God's forgiveness. Indeed, as we shall see in chapter seven, forgiveness is at the heart of our relationship with God.

We are not condemned to carry the burden of our guilt and shame for ever. Such feelings poison our lives, creating feelings of self-loathing that alienate us from ourselves and others. We are called, rather, to accept forgiveness and to start life anew.

Inner healing

Even when other people forgive us, we may not feel forgiven in our hearts. The words "you are forgiven" are not always enough to make us feel forgiven! A Catholic friend illustrates this very well:

> There was a time when I went to confession regularly. Each time, the priest absolved me! I was forgiven. For a few days, it was wonderful. And then, the old guilt, the old anxiety crept back in. I would go to confession again, recite the very same thing to a different priest, be forgiven again – and so the cycle went. I just couldn't feel forgiven.[2]

The heart of this friend's problem was that she could not forgive herself, and so could not believe that she was forgiven. To feel forgiven, to be truly healed of my transgressions, I must also forgive myself. That is to say, I must come to terms with what I have done, accept reality as it is and love myself unconditionally in that reality – warts and all. And that is hard to do.

Is it even *right* to love myself, no matter what I have done? Isn't that just letting myself off the hook? How can I be the judge of whether I have suffered enough, whether I have atoned adequately, whether I can be forgiven, when I myself am the sinner to be tried and forgiven? Such thoughts cut us off from forgiveness. But they rest in a misunderstanding of what forgiveness is, and how we can achieve it for ourselves.

To forgive yourself is not to let yourself "off the hook". On the contrary! True self-forgiveness involves a courageous and uncompromising acceptance of what you have done: of the damage caused, and the sheer wrongness of it all. True self-forgiveness begins with the recognition of the harm done, and with a genuine repentance for it. This painful acceptance is anything but letting yourself off the hook. It is a clear, stark acknowledgement of wrong. But to stay trapped in revulsion for my past behaviour serves no purpose. It puts nothing right. It leaves me fixated, perhaps obsessed by the past and with all that is wrong with me, all that I wish had been different, wish that I had done differently. It is right and proper to take responsibility for what we have done, for the person we have been, right and proper to grieve for our mistakes, and repent them. But it is right and proper to move on from there, to learn the lessons of the past and to become a better person as a consequence.

How many times do we vow that the victim of some outrage cannot be allowed to have suffered in vain, that lessons must be learned, that something good must come from this? The need to rise above pointless evil and create something better is a powerful human urge. It's easy to apply this urge when we are the victims. Surely, the need to apply it is stronger still, when we ourselves are the transgressor? What could create a more powerful urge to learn the lessons of the past and to do better than the recognition that we have offended – and that it is in our power to prevent the offence ever recurring?

The greatest act of atonement, of restitution, of repentance, is the turning away from wrongdoing towards a better way of being. This is the heart of self-forgiveness, the truth that justifies self-forgiveness. It is our new self, the self who is turning away from wrongdoing, that we can love, the new self who has had the courage to face – and repent – wrongdoing, the courage to try for something better.

If we focus on the past, on all that we have done wrong, it can be very hard to love ourselves. Focused on our wrongdoing we are consumed with self-loathing. But the past is gone! Inner healing comes from recognising this fact and switching our gaze to the present moment. And in that present moment, we may be loveable again. It is in this renewed self-love that we *experience* forgiveness and healing, that we accept that we are forgiven.

Ongoing change: conversion

Self-forgiveness is profoundly healing. In fact, it is essential to our sense of well-being. For if I cannot forgive myself, how can I value or nurture myself? Instead, I will punish and wound myself. This is no basis for new and healthy growth! Growth comes in the light of hope and acceptance, not in the darkness of rejection and despair. Inner healing alone can put us on the path of light and hope.

But self-forgiveness involves a great deal more than mere inner healing. In fact, it is a powerful vehicle for spiritual growth, a vehicle we all need. By conscientiously and continuously acknowledging our need for forgiveness, confessing and repenting our imperfections, and receiving forgiveness for them, we begin to embrace our better self.

Doing it over and over again

Catholics are often criticised for "cheating". "You Catholics! You behave as badly as anyone else, then you nip off to confession, you get absolution and come up smelling of roses – and then you go off and do it all again, confident that you will be forgiven again next week!"

It's hard to know how to answer such criticism. Of course, our need for forgiveness, our need for self-forgiveness and inner healing, is not a one-off thing. We don't, unfortunately, sin just the once, repent and become saints! In fact, we don't even come to a full understanding of just what it is that we should repent for in one blinding flash of insight. The fact is that our human understanding is slender and fragile. We are like people walking through darkness with only a small torch: we have battled the path behind us, tussled with some of its vagaries and come to some degree of understanding of it. But what lies ahead is a mystery. Only a fragment of the path is illuminated for us, a small pool of light that we know shows only a fraction of what is there. All we know is that there is more beyond, that we cannot yet see.

And so, yes, it is true, there will always be things I want to bring to confession. And indeed the things I bring to confession may not vary much. There are besetting sins, sins that reflect deep elements of my character, sins that come naturally to me. Try as I might, I make the same mistake again and again ... until my struggles finally create a breakthrough. But neither I nor the priest is satisfied by my continuing failure: would I express repugnance for something I wanted to continue? Would he absolve me, were I not repentant? Confession is no cheap salve for the soul, no empty ritual.

To imagine that the process of confession is a trite acknowledgment of our flaws, some kind of fatalistic acceptance that we will inevitably make the same mistake again, is a gross misunderstanding. The aim of confession, the aim of self-forgiveness, is far greater than that: it is no less than conversion.

Conversion and change

The archetype of conversion is the experience of St Paul. The story of his conversion from vicious persecutor of Christians to leading light of the Christian Church is legendary. In one blinding flash of light, one supreme experience, Paul's life and outlook were changed for ever.

For some people, conversion may be like that: a sudden blinding inspiration that changes everything for ever. For most of us, conversion is a slower, steadier process. In the Christian context, conversion – not material achievement – is the paradigm of life. Donald Gelpi, a Jesuit theologian, defines conversion as "the decision to reject irresponsible choices and to assume responsibility for one's subsequent development in some area of human experience".[3]

What exactly is conversion? It is the gradual, steady progress of insight and awareness of the consequences of our actions, our need for forgiveness, coupled with the valiant determination to learn from our mistakes, to seek out the higher path and to find ways to follow it. The process of conversion is nothing less than the process of being transformed from base clay into something exalted: from careless, insensitive or even evil-minded wrongdoing to awareness of goodness; from base motive to the imitation of Christ.

How is so radical a transformation of conversion to be achieved? Let's look again at the process of forgiveness, which is at the heart of the journey to conversion. That process of forgiveness applies, just the same, whether we are trying to forgive someone else or ourselves.

First, to begin the process of forgiveness, we must overcome denial. We must learn to look starkly, courageously, without excuse, at what we have done or failed to do. We must use every resource at our disposal to face the facts honestly. Initially, our ability to understand may be limited – we may only see the transgressions our consciousness is ready to see. But through repeated practice, through effort and openness to learning, we will progressively see more and more of the implications of our behaviour. The first stage of conversion is a matter of enlightenment about the effects of our actions.

Now, painfully, we must blame ourselves. Can I escape that blame? Of course, my behaviour reflects the culture around me, the way I have been treated, educated by others! *Of course*, in some senses, I am the innocent product of a time and place, of a particular history. But to leave it at that is to define myself as no more than flotsam, tossed about willy-nilly in the ocean of human affairs. A popular fridge magnet says: "Some days you're the insect, some days you're the windscreen" – as if whether we destroy or are destroyed is a matter of chance, happenstance, random accident. There's a grain of truth in that view: we are less in control of our destiny than we suppose. But there is a vast error, too, for happenstance, chance, random accident are excuses that remove all responsibility from us. Am I responsible for my actions? Yes, of course. Always. We are not automatons, you and I! There is always a degree of choice in how we act, in how we react to events.

Accepting responsibility for our actions is a giant step in maturity. In accepting responsibility we become adult, adult players in our complex universe, players who have the power to change things. And what we can most easily change is ourselves. Indeed, what we most need to change is ourselves.

Conversion is, fundamentally, a commitment to learning from past experiences and mistakes, learning how to be better, and committing oneself to that. Every day brings new mistakes! New opportunities to learn and develop.

And it is that word, develop, that most captures the power of confession, the power of conversion and the power of self-forgiveness that drives both confession and conversion. Only those who wish to transcend their present behaviour are motivated to confess, to repent the past, to develop beyond their present limitations. Only those who are ready to work for conversion, to receive the grace of being born anew, can truly transcend the past and achieve self-forgiveness.

Opening the door to spirituality

In each act of offering forgiveness, I affirm that a wrongdoer has a value that transcends particular actions or events: a value that transcends bodily existence or psychological characteristics or behaviour. In sum, in offering forgiveness, I affirm the spiritual value of the wrongdoer, and lift my gaze from his or her shortcomings to the true, best self that lies within. That wrongdoer may be another person, or it may be myself.

By affirming this spiritual value, particularly my own spiritual value, I open the door to spiritual awareness, and to the possibility of realising the best that is within me. I receive this gift of forgiveness because I repent, because I commit myself to strive for something better, something that will better reflect and be worthy of my true spiritual self. Self-forgiveness heals my wounds, but it also commits me to working for conversion, for spiritual enlightenment and growth. At the heart of that growth is love: unconditional love. In offering true forgiveness to another, there are no chains, no liabilities, no debits: the forgiveness is unconditional. In offering forgiveness to myself, acceptance of the past and healing for its wounds are equally unconditional. Forgiveness is an expression of love: of our love for ourselves, for others, a love that is a reflection of God's love for us.

EXERCISE

- Centre yourself, using the techniques we learned in the first chapter of this book.

- Bring yourself to bodily stillness and now ask yourself:
  What is there that I need to be forgiven for? How can I find that forgiveness? How can I forgive myself, and receive that forgiveness in my heart?

- Now focus again on your breathing.

- And bring yourself gently back to the world.

Recognising our own need to be forgiven is a powerful step. Recognising that forgiveness is truly possible, that it is truly healing, is a more powerful step still.

Notes

1   Correspondence to the authors.
2   Correspondence to the authors.
3   Donald Gelpi, *Grace as Transmuted Experience and Social Process and Other Essays in North American Theology* (Lanham, MD: University Press of America, 1988), 102.

7

The grace to forgive: a Catholic perspective

"May all of us who share in the body and blood of Christ
be brought together in unity by the Holy Spirit."
The Roman Missal: The Second Eucharistic Prayer

We have examined in some detail the human processes involved in forgiving – the emotions of anger, the challenge of letting go of resentment, the willingness to be freed from bitterness and the readiness to be reconciled with the offender if that would be safe. At this stage people often ask Catholic writers, be they psychologists or priests, whether faith in God or in the Church makes any difference to the process of forgiveness. Where does the grace of God feature in all this? Our response is that the grace of God is in the human process. The grace of God doesn't act on us from without: it works in us from within, from within the psychological laws and processes. God created those laws and processes and God's grace within us enables those processes of our nature to achieve our wholeness and growth.

Grace builds on nature
The Catholic Church doesn't have a two-tier view of humanity, viz. a natural and a supernatural tier. An ancient maxim in theology expresses this well, "grace builds on nature", or "grace presupposes nature". We cannot have a purely natural or a purely supernatural view of forgiveness because the human being doing the forgiving is at the same time natural and supernatural. All the natural processes that we have examined in this book are integral to the work of grace. It is never a question of, now that grace has taken over, the human processes can be dispensed with. Rather, it is always a question of how does grace inform, heal, revitalise and ensure that the human struggle leads to wholeness and growth.

But the question, "where does grace fit into all this?" has validity and is based on a deep intuition. How does a person who believes that he or she is forgiven by God forgive others? Does faith in God's forgiveness of oneself motivate us or facilitate us or make the act of forgiving others easier or more unconditional?

Individualistic notions of salvation

Our biggest problem lies with the excessively individualistic notions we all tend to hold about our relationship with God. Some of us, for instance, see ourselves as loved and forgiven by God, as isolated individuals, without real relationships with others. We have no concept of what it means to be "the Church", or to be "members of the Church". We have what has been described as a "me and Jesus mentality". Jesus loves and forgives me and that is all that matters! The fact that Jesus has asked us to live out this forgiveness within a whole new set of relationships doesn't impinge on our religious consciousness. As Christians we live in the religious awareness that we are God's forgiven people, called to live in the grace of forgiveness, and in the power of the Holy Spirit to share this grace with friend and foe alike.

Definition of the Church

The classic definition of the Church revived by the Second Vatican Council provides a starting point for a discussion of the Catholic understanding of forgiveness. The Council said that the Church is "a people made one with the unity of the Father, the Son and the Holy Spirit".[1] This "being made one" is what we mean by redemption. The sin that alienated us from God, from one another and even from ourselves is forgiven and removed in what Jesus called "a new birth". This new birth, the gift of our baptism, established us not only in a new relationship with the Father, Son and Holy Spirit, but also in a new relationship with one another. We become sons and daughters of God and sisters and brothers of one another.

This new relationship becomes embodied in our daily life and manifests itself in the new ways in which we live: hatred is replaced by love, resentment by forgiveness, meanness by generosity, deceit and double-dealing by truthfulness and honesty.

The Christian life is an organic whole. The wholeness and holiness of that life find concrete expressions in individual acts of love, forgiveness, truthfulness and justice. Just as a person who is a liar has to undergo a fundamental conversion before he or she becomes a truthful person, so a person who is an inveterate hater has to undergo a similar radical conversion before he or she becomes a loving and forgiving person. Our pastoral concern should always be with the underlying orientation of the person's life, with the fundamental option in life, and not simply with the isolated, individual act. If a person is not a loving person, and that always includes a healthy love of self, he or she will not be able to forgive. On the other hand, the person who is living the life of love and forgiveness will make this new life concrete in many individual acts of loving kindness and generous forgiveness each day and in so doing will live according to Jesus' command: "Be merciful, just as your Father is merciful" (Luke 6:36).

Priority of God's forgiveness
When we consider our relationship with God we recognise the priority of God's forgiveness over our repentance. We don't merit God's forgiveness through our repentance. Rather, as we open our hearts to receive God's forgiveness we undergo repentance. We seek to live a new life, free from sin and from the destructive effects of sin – jealousy, pride, sloth, lust, envy etc. God didn't wait for us to repent before forgiving us. God's offer of forgiveness is unconditional and, as we reach out to receive it, our hearts are changed. If we resist that change of heart we cannot appropriate or assimilate the forgiveness of God even if we spend hours on our knees.

Our forgiveness of one another is patterned by the Father's forgiveness of us. This is both the grace and the motivation for Christian forgiveness. We have a beautiful formulation of the Father's forgiveness in the prayer of absolution in the sacrament of reconciliation: "God the Father of mercies, through the death and resurrection of his Son Jesus Christ, has reconciled the world to himself and has sent the Holy Spirit among us for the forgiveness of our sins." Just as God doesn't wait for our repentance before forgiving us, neither do we wait for the repentance of the offender before we forgive him or her. If our offender receives our forgiveness he or she will have a change of heart. If our offender doesn't receive our forgiveness he or she will remain rooted in the offence. But we have done the Godlike thing. Now we are being "compassionate as our heavenly Father is compassionate". And the fact that the offender refuses to change doesn't diminish our Christ-like behaviour in any way. In fact it leads on to Christ's most radical formulation:

> But I say to you, Love your enemies and pray for those who persecute you, so that you may be children of your Father in heaven; for he makes his sun rise on the evil and on the good, and sends rain on the righteous and on the unrighteous. For if you love those who love you, what reward do you have? Do not even the tax collectors do the same? And if you greet only your brothers and sisters, what more are you doing than others? Do not even the Gentiles do the same? Be perfect, therefore, as your heavenly Father is perfect. (Matthew 5:44-48)

Matthew penned this command of the Lord within the experience of the disciples who were at the time being rejected and persecuted, just as Jesus was. This Gospel passage was a call to live as Jesus lived, to imitate him in the way in which he loved and forgave to the end.

Forgiving the unrepentant

We can easily empathise with a person who feels that he or she is justified in not forgiving if the offender refuses to apologise. After I had given two talks on forgiveness to priests, during their retreat, a retired Canon who was also a theologian said to me, "I would never forgive anyone who didn't ask for my forgiveness." When I asked him how he would reconcile his position with the teaching of Jesus he quoted what Jesus said in St Luke's Gospel: "If another disciple sins, you must rebuke the offender, and if there is repentance, you must forgive. And if the same person sins against you seven times a day, and turns back to you seven times and says, 'I repent,' you must forgive" (Luke 17:4). Certainly in this one passage of the Gospel Jesus talks about how to respond to a person who says he or she is sorry. But in the other passages Jesus talks about how we respond to those who wrong us without any reference to their repentance. So, when he teaches us how to pray he tells us to say, "forgive us as we forgive them". He doesn't add, "provided they say they are sorry"!

When a brother or sister wrongs us and comes to us and asks for forgiveness we grant it and, at the same time, we are reconciled with them. As the theologian Gregory Jones writes, "Christian forgiveness is the way God's love moves towards reconciliation and restoration of communion in the wake of sin."[2] In the absence of repentance, communion will not be restored. But the same forgiveness that is offered to the repentant brother or sister is also on offer even to the unrepentant enemy who would deny any relationship with us. That is why Jesus says to us, "love your enemies". And without any reference at all to their repentance Jesus says, "For if you forgive others their trespasses, your heavenly Father will also forgive you; but if you do not forgive others, neither will your Father forgive your trespasses" (Matthew 6:14-15).

Forgiving the unrepentant may seem to imply lack of concern for the destructive behaviour of others. There is, however, no incompatibility between forgiving from the heart and holding the forgiven person to account as, we hope, this book has made clear. I cannot take responsibility for their lack of accountability. At the same time I should never allow their refusal to be accountable to cause me to forgo the healing and liberating grace of forgiving them. That would only harm myself. So long as they remain unrepentant, reconciliation will not take place. But I am not responsible for their unrepentance: I am only responsible for my forgiveness. And, as long as I remain forgiving, I am living in a responsible way in my relationship with the unrepentant. I am being compassionate as my heavenly Father is compassionate.

A Christian Armenian witness

Christians through the ages have witnessed to this love of enemies. A well-known story from the Armenian Church, which suffered a horrible genocide in the early part of the twentieth century, at the hands of their Turkish enemies, illustrates this love in action:

> A Turkish officer raided and looted an Armenian home. He killed the aged parents and gave the daughters to the soldiers, keeping the eldest daughter for himself. Some time later she escaped and trained as a nurse. As time passed, she found herself nursing in a ward of Turkish officers. One night, by the light of a lantern, she saw the face of this officer. He was so gravely ill that without exceptional nursing he would die. The days passed, and he recovered. One day, the doctor stood by the bed with her and said to him, "But for her devotion to you, you would be dead." He looked at her and said, "We have met before, haven't we?" "Yes," she said, "we have met before." "Why didn't you kill me?" he asked. She replied, "I am a follower of him who said 'Love your enemies.'"[3]

The sacramental dimension of Christian forgiveness

In our profession of faith, as found in the Apostles' Creed, we say, "I believe in the Holy Spirit, the holy catholic Church, the communion of saints, the forgiveness of sins, the resurrection of the body, and the life everlasting." In the Creed we associate the forgiveness of sins with our faith in the Holy Spirit, the Church and the communion of saints. Jesus himself linked the forgiveness of sins with the Holy Spirit and baptism. On Easter Sunday evening, after his resurrection from the dead, he said to his disciples, "Receive the Holy Spirit. If you forgive the sins of any, they are forgiven them; if you retain the sins of any, they are retained" (John 20:22-23). And when he commissioned his disciples to go out and preach he said to them, "Go into all the world and proclaim the good news to the whole creation. The one who believes and is baptised will be saved" (Mark 16:15-16). Acting on this mission that the Lord gave them, the disciples went out to preach. In response to St Peter's first sermon in Jerusalem the people said, "Brothers, what should we do?" Peter answered, "Repent, and be baptised every one of you in the name of Jesus Christ so that your sins may be forgiven; and you will receive the gift of the Holy Spirit" (Acts 2:37-38).

The first sacrament of forgiveness
As the *Catechism of the Catholic Church* says, "Baptism is the first and chief sacrament of forgiveness of sins because it unites us with Christ, who died for our sins and rose for our justification, so that 'we too might walk in newness of life'."[4] Our baptism is a new birth, our spiritual birth as the sons and daughters of God our Father. In our baptism all our sins were taken away. Not only that, we were filled with the Holy Spirit and we were given the spiritual capacity to live a new way of life, a life that would mirror the life of Christ. In our baptism we became so united to Christ that the only image St Paul could use to describe this union is taken from the human body. He said, "For just as the body is one and has many members, and all the members of the body, though many, are one body, so it is with Christ. For in the one Spirit we were all baptised into one body – Jews or Greeks, slaves or free – and we were all made to drink of one Spirit" (1 Corinthians 12:12-13). We are the body of Christ: Christ is the head, we are the members. Together, we are the whole Christ.

Christ acting in us

It is in and through us that Christ is present in the world. It is in and through us that people encounter the loving and forgiving presence of Christ in their lives. St John Eudes, who died in 1680, expressed this mystical truth very clearly:

> Remember that our Lord Jesus Christ is your true head and that you are his members. He is to you as the head is to the members of the body; all that is his is yours. His spirit, his heart, his body, his soul, all his faculties, all are to be used by you as if they were your own, so that serving him you may praise him, love him, glorify him. For your part, you are to him as a member to the head, and he earnestly desires to use all your faculties as if they were his own for the service and glorification of his Father.[5]

Recall the story of Michael McGoldrick in chapter one. Michael wrote, "suddenly a picture of the crucified Christ came into my mind. It hit me that God's Son too had been murdered – for us". In that mystical moment Michael was transformed. The spiritual power of his baptism, his deep union with Christ, changed his life for ever and he could say, "Since Michael's death, I have been a changed man ... I feel as if Christ has taken hold of my life and I now want to take hold of Christ and give my life to loving God and serving people." Michael had discovered that through his union with Christ in baptism he has the power to love and forgive as Christ does. He can now say with St Paul, "I have been crucified with Christ; and it is no longer I who live, but it is Christ who lives in me" (Galatians 2:19-20).

Had Michael not been living in union with Christ he would not have had, in all probability, that mystical experience. But, in the time of his grief and despair, his living faith quickened within him the healing and liberating power of his baptism and enabled him to forgive. He discovered experientially the transforming power of the baptismal grace through which he had been reborn. He didn't have to work himself up to make a stoical effort to forgive. His forgiveness, like

Christ's forgiveness, was a sacrificial act of love. The numbing pain of his loss was still there, but the transforming power of grace made it possible for him to combine both the pain of loss and the love of forgiveness. Those who have never experienced this transforming reality of our baptismal grace at work in their lives may never understand how this can happen.

St Paul, in all his writings, ponders the deep mystery of our baptism through which we are joined to Christ. He says:

> So if anyone is in Christ, there is a new creation: everything old has passed away; see, everything has become new! All this is from God, who reconciled us to himself through Christ, and has given us the ministry of reconciliation; that is, in Christ God was reconciling the world to himself, not counting their trespasses against them, and entrusting the message of reconciliation to us. So we are ambassadors for Christ, since God is making his appeal through us; we entreat you on behalf of Christ, be reconciled to God. (2 Corinthians 5:17-20).

The role of the Holy Spirit in our lives

It is God who has reconciled us to himself, not as individuals in isolation, but by making us members of his people, the Church. And it is within the Church that we experience the forgiveness of our sins through the cleansing grace of the Holy Spirit. Speaking about how Christ founded his Church, Vatican II focused on the role of the Holy Spirit: "After being lifted up on the cross and glorified, the Lord Jesus poured forth the Spirit whom he had promised, and through whom he has called and gathered together the people of the New Covenant, which is the Church, into a unity of faith, hope and charity, as the Apostle teaches us."[6] The Council taught that the Church is the direct result of Christ's action of sending the Spirit. The primary role of the Holy Spirit is the sanctification of God's people, enabling us to live like Christ. As the theologian Tom Smail puts it:

The distinctive work of the Spirit is to communicate to us the life that is in the Father and the Son, so that we actually share and experience it in ourselves. In the Spirit the life that the Father wills and that the Son incarnates is brought over to our side of our relationship with them and begins to reach its destination in us as the first fruits of the whole human race for which it was intended.[7]

When the Spirit of God comes to dwell in us at our baptism it fills us with the whole life of God. We are, in the words of Jesus, "born of water and Spirit" (John 3:5). We become the people of the New Covenant, people empowered to love and forgive.

The Holy Spirit is the New Covenant

Over seven hundred years ago, St Thomas Aquinas clearly identified the New Covenant with the Holy Spirit. He wrote: "The New Covenant consists in the in-pouring of the Holy Spirit."[8] In another commentary he said: "As the Holy Spirit works in us charity which is the fullness of the Law, he himself is the New Covenant."[9] God promised to write the law of the New Covenant on our hearts: "This is the covenant I will make with the house of Israel ... I will put my law within them, and I will write it on their hearts" (Jeremiah 31:33). St Thomas quotes St Augustine, who said: "What else are the divine laws written by God himself on our hearts but the very presence of his Holy Spirit." In this same article St Thomas says: "that which is preponderant in the law of the New Covenant and whereon all its efficacy is based, is the grace of the Holy Spirit, which is given through faith in Christ. Consequently the New Law is chiefly the grace itself of the Holy Spirit."[10] Because the new law is chiefly the grace of the Holy Spirit, St Thomas says that, unlike the old law, the new law justifies us. It makes us holy because the law itself is the very presence of the sanctifying Holy Spirit. And when we live and act within the New Covenant we live and act in the Holy Spirit.

We are the "people of the New Covenant". That means, we are the people of the Holy Spirit, the people whose interior law of action is the

Spirit of God. As Fr Lyonnet wrote, "The law of the Spirit is by its very nature radically different from the old law. It is no longer a code, even if 'given by the Holy Spirit', but a law 'accomplished in us by the Holy Spirit'; not a simple, external norm of action, but what no other code of laws as such could be, a principle of action, a new, interior dynamism."[11] The new law is the sanctifying, dynamic presence of the Holy Spirit enabling us to be "compassionate as our heavenly Father is compassionate", to forgive as Christ forgives. That is why St Paul can say, "If we live by the Spirit, let us also be guided by the Spirit" (Galatians 5:25).

Our Christian morality is not a slavish following of laws; it is a joyful, free response to the Spirit of God who wants to transform us into the perfect image of Christ. (See Romans 8:29.) It is because we have this new dynamic source of spiritual energy within us through our baptism that we can now love and forgive as Jesus does. It is Jesus himself who lives and loves and forgives in us: "Jesus desires that all that is in him may live and hold sway in you; his spirit in your spirit, his heart in your heart, all the powers of his soul in those of your soul."[12]

Grace and forgiveness

The question regarding the relationship between the grace and the process of forgiveness takes on a new dimension when we accept our baptismal union with Christ. And it is not only the great saints who have this union. Each baptised person is brought into this same, profound union with Christ. Indeed, the Second Vatican Council said that "by his incarnation, he, the Son of God, has in a certain way united himself with each individual".[13]

Each human being has the power of Christ, God's power, for living a good life. Christ himself is praying for us. As we say in the penitential rite of the Mass, "you are pleading for us now at the right hand of the Father". Not only that, the Holy Spirit is praying within us. Writing to the Romans, St Paul said, "For all who are led by the Spirit of God are children of God. For you did not receive a spirit of slavery to fall back into fear, but you have received a spirit of adoption. When we cry, 'Abba! Father!' it is that very Spirit bearing witness with our spirit that we are children of God" (Romans 8:14-16).

The Spirit is Christ's first gift to us. The Spirit within us enables us to acknowledge what Christ has achieved for us: "But to all who received him, who believed in his name, he gave power to become children of God" (John 1:12). We acknowledge that we have become children of God through Christ when we call God "Father". When we say "Father" then the Spirit and our spirit bear united witness that we are children of God. And when we call God "Father" we are accepting one another as God's own children.

We need the Spirit in order to pray "Abba, Father". But we also need the Spirit to acknowledge that Jesus is Lord. St Paul says, "No one can say 'Jesus is Lord' except by the Holy Spirit" (1 Corinthians 12:3). Our human reason alone cannot give us the assurance that we are children of God. This assurance can only come through the Spirit. The Spirit brings to our consciousness the awareness that we are God's children and prays within us: Abba, Father. Tom Smail has made the fine distinction: we must pray this prayer for ourselves, but we cannot pray it by ourselves. None of us can decide, simply by our own reason, to accept God as our loving Father. That acceptance, that recognition, comes from the presence of the Holy Spirit in our hearts.

In the same way, the Spirit also brings to our consciousness the fact that Jesus is now seated at the right hand of the Father and enables us to acknowledge this mystery by proclaiming "Jesus Christ is Lord". The confession of the Lordship of Jesus comes through the grace of the Spirit's personal presence in our hearts. Again, we must make this profession that Jesus is Lord for ourselves, but we cannot make it by ourselves. This profession is the work of grace. Without the grace of faith all the study in the world will not enable a person to proclaim that Jesus is Lord.

Two short phrases, then, highlight the major work of the Holy Spirit in our hearts: through the Holy Spirit we can call God our loving Father; through the same Spirit we can proclaim that Jesus, who died for us, is now Lord of all. The Holy Spirit is a praying presence in our hearts, constantly interceding for us. We should hold on with great confidence to what St Paul tells us about this praying activity of the Spirit in our hearts: "Likewise the Spirit helps us in our weakness; for we do not know how to pray as we ought, but that very Spirit intercedes with sighs too deep for words. And God, who searches the heart, knows what is the mind of the Spirit, because the Spirit intercedes for the saints according to the will of God" (Romans 8:26-27).

Our hearts are full of prayer, not our own prayer, and not our own very inadequate words of prayer, but the eternal prayer of the Holy Spirit, interceding for us and bringing our deepest needs to our loving Father. The Spirit produces in us the prayer which he produces in the heart of Jesus. Now, in the same Spirit we can pray with Jesus, "Abba, Father". And in the same Spirit we can love and forgive as Jesus does.

Living in this deep union with God our Father, aware that Jesus is interceding for us, and conscious that we have within us the power of the Holy Spirit, we have a new capacity and a new motivation for looking at "the enemy" and praying as Jesus prayed on the cross: "Father, forgive them." Our forgiveness of one another is the concrete manifestation of our baptismal life of union with the Father, the Son and the Holy Spirit. Our act of forgiving is never an isolated, first-time attempt to do something good; our forgiveness always manifests the deeper spiritual reality that through our baptism we have indeed become "a new creation" and that is why we can now live and love in this new way.

Sacrament of confirmation
Everything that baptism achieves within us by our divine adoption as God's beloved children and the forgiveness of our sins, by the grace of the indwelling Holy Trinity in our hearts, and by our becoming the

body of Christ, is taken up and strengthened and fortified in the sacrament of confirmation. Vatican II said:

> By the sacrament of Confirmation they are more perfectly bound to the Church and are endowed with the special strength of the Holy Spirit. Hence, as true witnesses of Christ, they are more strictly obliged both to spread and to defend the faith by word and deed.[14]

Confirmation gives us a special grace for witnessing to Christ, witnessing to the life that Christ lived, and that was a life of love and forgiveness. The confirmed Christian, therefore, has a special grace for forgiving just as Jesus forgives. The Jesus who teaches us to pray to God the Father with the words "forgive us as we forgive them" is giving us his Holy Spirit so that we can do that. We might, at times, say, "Lord, I can't do that" but, if we prayerfully listen in our hearts, we will hear the Lord say, "Let my Spirit do it in you and let me do it in you." When the Church celebrates the sacrament of confirmation it asks God for all the special graces and strengths which we need for our life of forgiving love.

Confirmation as the completion of baptism

Confirmation is the completion of baptism. In the early Church the two sacraments were not separated. Both were conferred at the same time. But, through a host of historical circumstances, the celebration of confirmation has been separated in time from the celebration of baptism. The *Catechism of the Catholic Church* succinctly states the nature of the issues involved in the early history of this separation:

> In the first centuries Confirmation generally comprised one single celebration with Baptism, forming with it a "double sacrament", according to the expression of St Cyprian. Among other reasons, the multiplication of infant baptisms all through the year, the increase of rural parishes and the growth of dioceses often prevented the bishop from being present at all baptismal celebrations. In the West the desire to reserve the completion of Baptism to the bishop caused the temporal separation of the two

sacraments. The East has kept them united, so that Confirmation is conferred by the priest who baptizes. But he can do so only with the *myron* consecrated by the bishop.[15]

There is an ongoing discussion in the Church today about this separation of baptism and confirmation. But for our purposes we want simply to draw attention to the powerful prayer that the bishop prays for all those presenting themselves for confirmation:

> All-powerful God, Father of our Lord Jesus Christ,
> by water and the Holy Spirit
> you freed your sons and daughters from sin
> and gave them new life.
> Send your Holy Spirit upon them
> to be their Helper and Guide.
> Give them the spirit of wisdom and understanding,
> the spirit of right judgement and courage,
> the spirit of knowledge and reverence.
> Fill them with the spirit of wonder and awe in your presence.
> We ask this through Christ our Lord.

In the sacrament of confirmation the whole Church prays that those who are being confirmed will be filled with the gifts of the Holy Spirit and thus be reinvigorated in their baptismal lives. I can say in my heart, "What I cannot do in my own power I can do in the power of the Holy Spirit." When facing a difficult situation I would be very ill advised to try and face it on my own, to act as if I were not a confirmed Christian. When I find myself in conflict with someone, whether with a friend or a foe, I need the wisdom for which the Church prayed when I was confirmed: "Give them the spirit of wisdom and understanding, the spirit of right judgement and courage." But in the heat of conflict, or in the midst of distractions, or in the weakness of our sinfulness we can easily forget to turn inward and find within our hearts the God who saves us. St Augustine described, in a classic text, how he discovered himself doing just that:

Too late have I loved you, O Beauty so ancient and so new, too late have I loved you! Behold, you were within me, while I was outside; it was there I sought you, and, a deformed creature, rushed headlong upon these things of beauty which you have made. You were with me, but I was not with you. They kept me far from you, those fair things which, if they were not in you, would not exist at all. You have called to me, and have cried out, and have shattered my deafness. You blazed forth with light, and have shone upon me, and you have put blindness to flight! You have sent forth fragrance, and I have drawn my breath, and I pant after you. I have tasted you, and I hunger and thirst after you. You have touched me, and I have burned for your peace.[16]

Augustine became aware not only that God was within, but also that he himself was without: "you were within me, while I was outside". If we do not dwell happily with God who is within us, we begin to live outside ourselves – escaping from the God within, but also escaping from ourselves. Then we are living as if we had never been confirmed. And while we are trying to escape from ourselves we will find it very hard to forgive and our faith will seem to be of no value at all. Our faith will seem powerless.

Sacrament of reconciliation

Very often a person may be trying to escape because they have been badly hurt. There is a great difference between the broken heart that feels paralysed when challenged to forgive and the hard heart which is determined not to forgive. The broken heart needs healing; the hard heart needs conversion. In the sacrament of reconciliation we have both the grace of healing and the grace of conversion. This difference is well illustrated by the following example of a zealous religious sister:

Early in 1970 I had experienced a great sadness for several months. It occurred because I was aware that a great injustice had been done to a wonderful lady who gave herself tirelessly to helping all of us in our organisation and the people we cared for. To me she exhibited all the qualities of true Christianity.

For whatever reason, the person in charge decided to cause untold pain to this lady, by undermining her in cruel language. All this lady had been doing (and continued to do on a voluntary basis) was to help the smooth running of the organisation and to alleviate myself and others (who were overworked) of many duties.

Because this lady was such a nice person she wouldn't let me say anything to the offending person. Therefore I found myself in this terrible boiling angry space inside. I found it very difficult to be civil to the person in charge when I met her and had to do business, and as we shared the same premises this was a constant occurrence.

I was blessed with the opportunity to follow the three months' renewal course at Hawkstone Hall. During the course we had a week dedicated to looking at the ministry of healing which culminated in a service of prayer for individual healing.

I asked Fr Jim to pray for the gift to forgive this person. I approached this situation with a certain ambivalence. During the prayer I felt a sense of deep peace descending on me like a cloak, freeing my whole body and filling my heart with joy. From that day on I was freed from my intense anger towards this person. And as time progressed I began to feel compassion towards the woman, happy to do many kindnesses for her. I haven't forgotten the incident but it has no power over me and I look back on it as a cause of great blessing for me. Praise the Lord.[17]

This sister's testimony makes it clear that sometimes very good and loving people have a long struggle with forgiveness, not because they don't want to forgive, but because they have been so deeply hurt that they feel incapable of forgiving. Before she could forgive she had first to experience inner healing.

The sacrament of reconciliation, better known as confession, has always been seen as the sacrament of second conversion. Baptism is the sacrament of first conversion when we are reborn of the Holy Spirit and all our sins are forgiven; confession is the sacrament of "second conversion", the gift of Christ through which our sins are forgiven and the wounds inflicted by sin are healed.

On Easter Sunday evening the risen Lord said to his disciples, "Receive the Holy Spirit. If you forgive the sins of any, they are forgiven them; if you retain the sins of any, they are retained" (John 20:22-23). The Church's faith crystallised into the firm belief that the Easter gift of the risen Lord, namely the power to forgive sins through the Holy Spirit, remains with the Church. It remains, as we have seen in the sacrament of baptism but also in the sacrament of reconciliation. It is said that when someone asked the great G. K. Chesterton why he became a Catholic he said it was because he wanted someone to use the power Jesus gave to the Church and say to him, "Your sins are forgiven." The desire to hear the forgiveness of God proclaimed through the power of the Holy Spirit is one of the deepest desires of the sinful heart.

The experience of the Church throughout the centuries has been that a good confession brings great peace to the soul. The great Redemptorist moral theologian Bernard Häring described peace:

> The Biblical concept of peace is amazingly comprehensive. It includes salvation, wholeness, integrity, healthy and healing interpersonal relationships, cultural, economic and social relationships and transformations which serve the cause of peace and of wholeness and integrity.[18]

God's gift of peace is lost through serious sin. If we knowingly and willingly do what is contrary to God's will our soul is bereft of peace. Only God's gift of forgiveness, received through our contrite confession, restores our peace. While the peace of soul is lost through serious sin, our peace can be disturbed by what the *New Rite of Penance* calls "the wound of sin".[19]

Healing the wound of sin

In the introduction to the *New Rite of Penance* we read: "Just as the wounds of sin are varied and multiple in the life of individuals and of the community, so too the healing which penance provides is varied."[20]

We recognise two effects of sin: sin as an offence against God – causing an alienation between God and self and the wound of sin – the inner hurt caused in a person by the sinful action or words of others. The sin itself will be manifested in a cold, deliberate, malicious act of one kind or another; the wound of sin will reveal itself through some kind of reaction. Just as a person in pain may cry out, so a person with the wound of sin may very well "strike out". For the sin itself we need God's forgiveness; for the wound of sin we need the Lord's healing. Both are signified in the words of absolution: "Through the ministry of the Church may God give you pardon and peace." Pardon is for the sin; peace is for the wound of sin.

New emphasis in the sacrament of reconciliation[21]

The healing of the wound of sin is the new emphasis in our understanding of the sacrament of reconciliation. The Church always saw the sacrament as the great means of forgiveness. We did not, however, always focus on the healing power of the sacrament. If a husband and wife, for instance, have a nasty row and they do not take time to show each other loving forgiveness, the hurts which they have inflicted on one another will remain unhealed. Very little provocation will be needed to spark off the next row. If they continue in this cycle of fighting, without really healing the wounds through loving and tender forgiveness, they will reach a stage in their relationship where the slightest thing will provoke a row. They will not be able to communicate with each other; they will blame one another; they will no longer be able to trust one another. The breakdown in their relationship will be caused by the inner wounds which they have inflicted on each other and which have been allowed to fester. They may even be blaming each other for the lack of communication or trust, whereas the real cause will be the unhealed wounds.

If they bring their wounds to the sacrament of reconciliation they will experience healing. They will be able peacefully to face the task of rebuilding their relationship. While the wounds remain unhealed this task will be impossible for them. Forgiveness will seem impossible, and too risky. Even if only one of them seeks healing for the wound of sin the total relationship will be transformed. The healed partner will no longer be re-acting out the inner wound, but responding in love.

A woman was praying for God to do something about her husband. He had no faith and was reacting negatively to her strong faith. As she was asking God to change her husband for the better God let her see that by praying this prayer she was sitting in judgement on her husband. The Lord taught her to pray this prayer: "Lord, heal my marriage, but begin with me." She kept praying this prayer faithfully. She began to notice that her husband was going out on the same evening each week. He did not say where he was going. On his return one evening he took her completely by surprise and announced that he was about to be received into the Church. His mysterious weekly trips were for instruction in the faith. From the moment she began to take responsibility for their relationship and ask God to begin the healing of their marriage in her, their relationship improved. The whole relationship changed because she was willing to ask the Lord to heal the wounds in herself.

The sacrament of reconciliation is for the healing of all inner wounds. When a Catholic speaks to me about a painful or broken relationship I always suggest that we should bring the relationship to the celebration of the sacrament of reconciliation. In the celebration we listen to the word of God; we pray for discernment; we enter into deeper sorrow for sin; we confess our sins; we receive God's forgiveness for our sins and healing for the wounds of sins; in our purpose of amendment we promise God to do our best to avoid these sins and the occasion of sin in the future. When the inner wound has been healed he or she can look at the relationship with new eyes. Looking at the relationship from the place of inner pain may convince the person that forgiveness and reconciliation are out of the question. Once the inner wound, however, has been healed the person can review the relationship with new eyes. Forgiveness will be present and reconciliation might be possible. As the person seeks reconciliation with God in the sacrament he or she can be led to seek reconciliation with the person who has caused hurt and offence, if the human basis for such reconciliation exists.

While the psycho-therapeutic aim of forgiveness will always be the healing of the inner wound, the theological goal of forgiveness will always be reconciliation and the restoration of communion. Sometimes, however, as we made plain in the previous chapter, the goal of restored communion will not be reached in this life. But even if, humanly speaking, reconciliation would not be possible or advisable, forgiveness will always be possible and forgiveness will always bring a great blessing.

The specific gift of confession is this: people can bring all sins for which they are sorry to the sacrament, no matter how serious; they can confess them with the certainty that God forgives the sins and heals the wounds of sin, and they have the assurance that confidentiality is guaranteed. In the strictest sense they can come to the sacrament and unburden themselves. When they unburden themselves of their inability to forgive, the grace and power of the sacrament set them free. If their inability to forgive is caused by a hard and unforgiving heart, they will receive in the sacrament the grace of that deep conversion that God promises: "A new heart I will give you, and a new spirit I will put within you; and I will remove from your body the heart of stone and give you a heart of flesh" (Ezekiel 36:26). If their inability to forgive comes from a deeper inner wound they will receive inner healing in the sacrament. Jesus has come "to bind up the broken-hearted" (Isaiah 61:1).

The heart of the sacrament is the forgiving, sanctifying and healing presence of the Holy Spirit; Christ's Easter gift of the Spirit is for the forgiveness of our sins. It is also our divine physician's remedy for the wounds of sin. The sacrament, celebrated with contrition for sin, truly binds up the broken heart and enables us to enter into the new freedom that forgiveness brings.

The Holy Eucharist

Our most frequently celebrated sacrament is the Eucharist, the Mass. Each time we enter into the celebration of the mystery of the Mass we are invited, not only to ask God for forgiveness, but also to offer forgiveness to everyone in our own lives. We celebrate the Eucharist for the glory of God. St Irenaeus told us that the "glory of God is the human person fully alive". This means that when God is being glorified something is happening in us. We are being changed. Everything in us, which is in any way opposed to being fully alive in the Spirit, is being dealt with. If it is a sin, it is being forgiven; if it is a wound of sin, it is being healed; if it is a bondage of sin or evil, we are being set free. If we come to the Mass acknowledging bitterness and unforgiveness and asking God for forgiveness and freedom, we will be set free.

The Second Vatican Council reminded us that the Eucharist is at the very centre of our worship of God and our life as the people of God:

> The other sacraments, as well as every ministry of the Church and every work of the apostolate, are linked with the holy Eucharist and are directed towards it. For the most blessed Eucharist contains the Church's entire spiritual wealth, that is, Christ himself, our Passover and living bread. Through his very flesh, made vital and vitalising by the Holy Spirit, he offers life to men and women. They are thereby invited and led to offer themselves, their labours, and all created

things together with him. Hence the Eucharist shows itself to be the source and apex of the whole work of preaching the gospel.[22]

We know, with the instinct of faith, that the Mass is the most important act of worship in our life. In the Mass, perfect worship is offered to God our Father, because in the Mass it is Jesus Christ, our High Priest, who is offering himself to the Father. In his great encyclical letter on the Eucharist, Pope John Paul II said:

> The Church draws her life from the Eucharist. This truth does not simply express a daily experience of faith, but recapitulates the heart of the mystery of the Church. In a variety of ways she joyfully experiences the constant fulfilment of the promise: "And remember, I am with you always, to the end of the age" (Matthew 28:20), but in the Holy Eucharist, through the changing of bread and wine into the body and blood of the Lord, she rejoices in this presence with unique intensity. Ever since Pentecost, when the Church, the People of the New Covenant, began her pilgrim journey towards her heavenly homeland, the Divine Sacrament has continued to mark the passing of her days, filling them with confident hope.[23]

The Mass is the eternal sacrifice of Christ made present to us sacramentally under the species of bread and wine. The priest, as he extends his hands over the bread and wine, prays: "Let your Spirit come upon these gifts ... so that they may become for us the body and blood of our Lord, Jesus Christ." Just as Jesus was conceived in his mother's womb, by the power of the Holy Spirit, so through that same power, the bread and wine are transformed into his body and blood.

The presence of God

As we celebrate the Mass we enter into the presence of God. To prepare ourselves to enter into God's holy presence we acknowledge our sinfulness and we pray not just for pardon but also for healing. The awareness of our sinfulness and of our wounds makes us conscious of the healing power of Christ and we pray: "You were sent to heal the contrite. Lord, have mercy." Aware of the division caused by our sins, we confidently confess our sins and we pray: "Lord Jesus, you heal the wounds of sin and division. Christ, have mercy." While the Church seeks to make us conscious of our sinfulness right at the beginning of the Mass, we are also made aware of God's healing love. Throughout the Mass we grow in this awareness of our sinfulness, but we also experience a corresponding growth in our awareness of God's healing love, culminating in the great act of faith before communion when we cry out: "Lord, I am not worthy to receive you, but only say the word and I shall be healed." – my whole person, my whole being, in body, mind and spirit – I shall be healed. In the Mass, as we become conscious of our need for forgiveness, we hear the comforting words: this blood "will be shed for you and for all so that sins may be forgiven". With great confidence we pray: "Lord Jesus Christ ... look not on our sins, but on the faith of your Church." And with expectation in our hearts we cry out twice: "Lamb of God, you take away the sins of the world: have mercy on us." Still mindful of our sinfulness and our need for forgiveness, the priest prays: "Lord Jesus Christ, Son of the living God, by the will of the Father and the work of the Holy Spirit your death brought life to the world. By your holy body and blood free me from all my sins and from every evil. Keep me faithful to your teaching, and never let me be parted from you."

Having acknowledged our sinfulness many times throughout the Mass and asked God's forgiveness, we are now ready to receive Holy Communion. We should note that this recognition of sinfulness is not a depressive, "I am no good", stance before God. Rather, from the prayers we get a sense of grateful confidence in God's acceptance of us, even though we are sinners. The prayers are more about the fidelity of God than about our own unfaithfulness. As the theologian Ray Noll writes:

> ... it is no surprise that in both Hebrew and Greek and in church Latin the term "to confess one's sins" *also means* "to give praise to God". St Augustine in one of his homilies reminds his North

African Berber community that when the Latin Church prays "confitemur" we mean not just that we confess our sins to God but that we pour forth our praise to God as well.[24]

Forgiveness presumed as we share in the Eucharist
The Mass, offered for the glory of God, heals within us everything that is opposed to God's glory. In the Mass we have healing for all resentment, bitterness, selfishness and lack of forgiveness. But to receive that healing we must do what the Lord commands:

> So when you are offering your gift at the altar, if you remember that your brother or sister has something against you, leave your gift there before the altar and go; first be reconciled to your brother or sister, and then come and offer your gift. (Matthew 5:23-24)

If we do not seek reconciliation with a person we have hurt, God will not be glorified in our celebration, and there will be no healing. Sometimes, sadly, the other person doesn't want anything more to do with you. Then there can be no possibility – at least for the moment – of reconciliation. But you have done your best. The intention in your heart is to seek forgiveness for the wrong. When you share the sign of peace with others you are symbolising to all that you are seeking to live at peace with everyone, including the one who is refusing to forgive you.

In this distressing situation where someone refuses to be reconciled with you, you refrain from judgement. You acknowledge that the person is deeply hurt, and that while that hurt remains unhealed, he or she will not be able to accept your apology or your request for forgiveness. But you can enter into eucharistic communion with them even though they are excluding you from their friendship.

Participation in the Eucharist requires unconditional forgiveness for each person in our life. Conditional forgiveness is not the forgiveness that Christ speaks of when he says to Peter "seventy-seven times" (Matthew 18:22). Forgiveness withheld from a single person blocks the healing power of the Eucharist. Notice that in the penitential rite we prayed, "You were sent to heal the contrite." Jesus cannot heal those who are not contrite. The second Vatican Council was very aware of the need for forgiveness for a fruitful celebration of the liturgy when it said, "Before people can come to the liturgy they must be called to faith and conversion."[25]

In the celebration of the Mass we have "the Church's entire spiritual wealth". Everything that Christ has done for us is present in the mystery of the Mass. As the Vatican Council document says,

> At the Last Supper, on the night when he was betrayed, our Saviour instituted the eucharistic sacrifice of his body and blood. This he did in order to perpetuate the sacrifice of the Cross throughout the ages until he should come again, and so to entrust to his beloved spouse, the Church, a memorial of his death and resurrection: a sacrament of love, a sign of unity, a bond of charity, a paschal banquet in which Christ is consumed, the mind is filled with grace, and a pledge of future glory is given to us.[26]

Deeper union with Christ
During our celebration of the Eucharist we have the most opportune moment to act on Pope John Paul II's insight:

> Those who wish to understand themselves thoroughly – and not just in accordance with the immediate, partial, often superficial, and even illusory standards and measures of their being – they must with all their unrest, uncertainty and even their weakness and sinfulness, with their life and death, draw near to Christ. They must, so to speak, enter into him with their own self, they must "appropriate" and assimilate the whole reality of the Incarnation and the Redemption in order to find themselves. If this profound process takes place within them, they then bear fruit not only in adoration of God but also of deep wonder at themselves.[27]

In the Eucharist we have the complete reality of the incarnation and redemption present sacramentally on the altar. As we offer ourselves to God we open our whole lives to be filled with "all the fullness of God" (Ephesians 3:19). We share with everyone a sign that we have received his gift and that we want to share it. We are invited to offer each other a sign of peace. The Council tells us that the Eucharist is "a sacrament of love, a sign of unity, a bond of charity".[28] Holy Communion presupposes that I love and forgive my enemies; it assumes that I have confessed all grave sin and that I am sorry for all my sins; it implies that I am actively seeking unity and peace with everyone in my life.

A Christian witness from San Salvador

The Jesuit theologian Jon Sobrino gives us a wonderful example of how people of faith in a refugee camp in San Salvador saw the intrinsic connection between sharing in the Eucharist and forgiving their enemies:

> Around the altar on that day there were various cards with the names of family members who were dead or murdered. People would have liked to go to the cemetery to put flowers on their graves. But as they were locked up in the refuge and could not go, they painted flowers round their names. Beside the cards with the names of family members there was another card with no flowers which read: "Our dead enemies. May God forgive them and convert them." At the end of the Eucharist we asked an old man what was the meaning of this last card and he told us this: "We made these cards as if we had gone to put flowers on our dead because it seemed to us they would feel we were with them. But as we are Christians, you know, we believed that our enemies should be on the altar too. They are our brothers in spite of the fact that they kill us and murder us. And you know what the Bible says. It is easy to love our own but God asks us also to love those who persecute us."[29]

What a deep understanding of the Eucharist these people displayed! In the Mass we pray for the living and the dead. We cannot truly enter into the celebration of this mystery of the Lord's death and resurrection, of his forgiving his enemies just before he died, if we are not prepared to pray for our own enemies, whether alive or dead. Each time we join in the celebration of the Mass we are saying to the Church, "I want to forgive, I am willing to forgive, I need the grace to forgive."

EXERCISE

- Centre yourself, using the techniques we learned in the first chapter of this book.

- Bring yourself to bodily stillness and calm.

- Reflect on your baptismal union with Christ. He is one with you and invites you to become aware of your oneness with him.

- What hurts do you want to bring to the Lord? Can you mention them specifically to him?

- Which sacrament would best bring you healing for those hurts at this time?

- Are you ready to celebrate the sacrament for that healing?

- Now focus again on your breathing.

- And bring yourself gently back to the world.

You have the opportunity at any time to go to Mass and pray for all those who have hurt you or to go to Confession and bring all your own hurts to the Lord. You can find tremendous healing in these sacraments of our faith.

Notes

1   Second Vatican Council, *Lumen Gentium*, 4.
2   Gregory Jones, *Embodying Forgiveness: A Theological Analysis* (Grand Rapids, MI: W. B Eerdmans, 1995), 155.
3   Cited in Gregory Jones, *Embodying Forgiveness*, 265-266.
4   *Catechism of the Catholic Church*, 977.
5   St John Eudes, *The Adorable Heart of Jesus*, I, 5.
6   Second Vatican Council, *Unitatis Redintegratio*, 2.
7   Tom Smail, *The Giving Gift: The Holy Spirit in Person* (London: Darton, Longman and Todd, 1994), 167.
8   St Thomas Aquinas, "Commentary on Hebrews", cap. 8, lect. 2
9   St Thomas Aquinas, "Commentary on 2 Corinthians", cap. 3, lect. 2.
10   St Thomas Aquinas, *Summa Theologiae*, 1a, 2ae, Q. 106, art. 1.
11   Ignace de la Potterie and Stanislaus Lyonnet, *The Christian Lives by the Spirit* (Staten Island, NY: Alba House, 1971), 158.
12   St John Eudes, *The Adorable Heart of Jesus*, I, 5.
13   Second Vatican Council, *Gaudium et Spes*, 22.
14   Second Vatican Council, *Lumen Gentium*, 11.
15   *Catechism of the Catholic Church*, 1290.
16   *The Confessions of St Augustine* (translated with an introduction and notes by John K. Ryan; New York: Doubleday, 1960), book 10, chapter 27.
17   Correspondence to the authors.
18   Bernard Häring, *The Healing Power of Non-violence* (Slough: St Paul's Publications, 1986), 13.
19   *New Rite of Penance* (Dublin: Veritas, 1976), 7.
20   *New Rite of Penance*, 7.
21   For what follows in this section, see Jim McManus, *The Healing Power of the Sacraments* (Chawton: Redemptorist Publications, 2005)
22   Second Vatican Council, *Presbyterorum Ordinis*, 5.
23   John Paul II, *Ecclesia de Eucharistia* (London: CTS, 2003), 1.
24   Ray Noll, *Sacraments: A New Understanding for a New Generation* (Mystic, CT: Twenty-Third Publications, 1999), 113.
25   Second Vatican Council, *Sacrosanctum Concilium*, 9.
26   Second Vatican Council, *Sacrosanctum Concilium*, 47.
27   John Paul II, *Redemptor Hominis* (London: CTS, 1979), 10.
28   Second Vatican Council, *Sacrosanctum Concilium*, 47.
29   Jon Sobrino, "Latin America: Place of Sin and Place of Forgiveness", *Concilium*, 184 (1986), 50.

8

Finding forgiveness in prayer

*"God instituted prayer so as to confer upon his creatures
the dignity of being causes."*
Pascal

At the end of each chapter of this book we have invited you to take some time to get in touch with your inner self and to reflect on the mystery of your life as we were unfolding the process of forgiveness. In this final chapter we invite you to enter more deeply into a time of prayer. You have probably critically analysed what we have been saying in this book; you may have disagreed quite strongly with some of our opinions. On the other hand you may have agreed totally with our approach to the personal and spiritual work of forgiving and you may have been saying, "I wish I had read this twenty or thirty years ago." Whatever your attitudes and whatever your appraisal of our work, we want to give you the opportunity to bring the whole area of forgiveness to God in a personal time of prayer.

We will base our prayerful reflections on a most beautiful song of the praise of God's merciful love as found in Psalm 103.[1] We will read the psalm verse by verse, reflect on it, pray on it and allow it to speak to our hearts. We do this in the faith that the psalm is God's word spoken to us for our encouragement. The first verse of the psalm reads:

> My soul, give thanks to the Lord,
> all my being, bless his holy name.
> My soul, give thanks to the Lord
> and never forget all his blessings.

How to praise God
We are invited in this psalm to come in gratitude to God, with our whole being, with all that is within us, and bless his holy name. We are

directed to bless God, not just with pious thoughts and phrases, but with our whole being, with all that is within us.

What is within us? Everything that has ever happened in our whole life is within us. It is registered in that faculty that we call memory. But it is not only filed in memory, it is also imprinted on our character. You are the person you are at this moment because of all that you have lived through. Had you lived at a different time, in a different place, with a different occupation and with different experiences, you would not be the person you are right now. Your experiences have moulded you; the successes and failures of your life to date are part of the inner fabric of your being. When God's word in the psalm teaches you to say, "all my being, bless his holy name", you are being invited to praise God, not just for the successes but also for the failures. Which do you think have been more formative in your life? For which can you most heartily give thanks to God? All my being, bless his holy name. All the pain and all the joy, all the love and all the sorrow, all the virtue and all the vice, all the grace and all the sin. All that is within me, bless God's holy name. What a prayer God teaches us to pray! We are taught to praise him equally for the good and the bad.

Teaching of St Patrick

Centuries ago God taught the great evangelist St Patrick to praise him for all things and in all things. Patrick recorded this teaching for us. He wrote:

> I give thanks to my God tirelessly who kept me faithful in the day of trial, so that today I offer sacrifice to him confidently, the living sacrifice of my life to Christ, my Lord, who preserved me in all my troubles. I can say therefore: Who am I, Lord, and what is my calling that you should co-operate with me with such divine power? Today, among heathen peoples, I praise and proclaim your name in all places, not only when things go well but also in times of stress. Whether I receive good or ill, I return thanks equally to God, who taught me always to trust him unreservedly.[2]

God taught the great St Patrick how to relate to all the circumstances of his life. It is natural to be thankful to God when things are going well. But God taught Patrick to be equally thankful when things were going badly, when people were opposing him and trying to undermine his work. That goes against the grain of our selfishness.

Real prayer, deep worship in the spirit, calls forth within us gratitude to God for everything. That great mystic of the Middle Ages, Meister Eckhart, said, "If the only prayer a person said throughout the whole of life was 'thank you' he or she would have prayed very well." Gratitude lifts the heart above all the adversities of this life and enables us to transcend our selfish interests and points of view. Gratitude to God, even for adversaries, as St Patrick discovered, ensures that great good comes out of all adversity and failure. God's ambition for you is that you share his life here on earth and see and enjoy him for ever in heaven. Your failures may be as significant in your faith journey as your successes, and your enemies may contribute as much to you achieving your eternal destiny as your friends. That is why we pray "all my being, bless his holy name".

The God who forgives

Notice how God is preparing us for life's struggles in this psalm. God's first lesson to us is not about repenting or forgiving but about praising God's holy name in all things and for all things. The person that can praise God even for the enemy will not baulk at the thought of forgiving that same enemy nor will he or she shrink from rejoicing in the forgiveness that God offers. In the next verse of the psalm God assures us of his forgiveness and healing.

> It is he who forgives all your guilt,
> who heals every one of your ills,
> who redeems your life from the grave,
> who crowns you with love and compassion,
> who fills your life with good things,
> renewing your youth like an eagle's.

Having taught us to praise with all that is within us, God now lays before us his redeeming work in our lives. And God's first work of redemption is forgiveness: forgiveness for all our guilt. God takes away all our sins and removes all our guilt. But we have to cooperate with this saving grace. We can't be freed from guilt if we are holding on to it. Imagining that you are too bad, too guilty for even God to redeem, would be an extraordinary act of foolish pride. Can God's mercy match your guilt? Can God's compassion compete with your sense of worthlessness? St Bernard got it right when he said, "What I can't obtain by myself, I appropriate to myself with confidence from the pierced side of the Lord because he is full of mercy. The mercy of God, therefore, is my merit. And what about my righteousness? O Lord, I shall remember only your righteousness. It is also mine because you are God's righteousness for me."[3]

All my being, bless. We see the wisdom of God in teaching us first to praise him with all that is within us before God leads us to focus on what has been forgiven. If even my guilt and sin have already responded to this divine invitation to praise, then I will more easily let go of them. Why hold on to something that God wants to take away? God has forgiven you your sin. As you now turn to him in love and sorrow, you can let go of all your guilt. God's forgiveness is unconditional. Take a moment now in your heart to receive it. And as you open your heart to receive God's unconditional forgiveness don't be thinking about yourself – about what you have done, or not done, about your unworthiness or your guilt – think only about what God is doing. In this beautiful image God is telling you what he is doing: "I will sprinkle clean water upon you, and you shall be clean from all your uncleannesses, and from all your idols I will cleanse you. A new heart I will give you, and a new spirit I will put within you" (Ezekiel 36:25-26).

The God who heals
Not only does God forgive all our guilt, but also heals every one of our ills. In the context of human relationships our ills so often take the form

of betrayal: someone we love puts selfishness before the loyalty we expected or instead of the word of encouragement in a time of need we have been seared with the destructive word of criticism. A relationship that we may have thought unbreakable and inviolable was fractured and discarded; maybe in a world where we seemed to have everything we need for a happy life we lost the only thing that could bring us happiness, namely the love and friendship of a spouse or an intimate friend. Our deepest ills are never simply physical. Our deepest ills are always personal and spiritual, the loss of friendship with God or the pain of broken relationships.

But God assures you that every one of your ills is healed". There is no inner pain that God wants you to hold in the secret of your heart without bringing it to God in love and confidence. If you have been betrayed or rejected, if a former friend has turned against you and now has become an enemy, if you seem cut off from all your loved ones and have no friends, if you feel all alone in the world, God will hear the cry of your heart when you turn to him. But you have to turn with trust and love. Unfortunately when you are rejected by a friend you may subtly begin to reject God or blame God and deep down, without ever verbalising it, begin to feel that it was all God's fault. God wants to "heal every one of your ills". But you have to bring them into God's presence.

So often our "ills" have a face, the face of our betrayer or our one-time friend who has become our enemy. That face can invade our inner self at any time. So long as that face is there it is part of all that is within you. And, in the first part of the psalm, we were taught to call upon that face to bless God's holy name. The healing of our ills that God offers can only happen when our ills begin to bless God. So often I have seen people crippled by the face of their ill, haunted night and day by the face of their betrayer. They were living in despair of ever being free from this nightmare. Then when they began to live by this word of God and bless God, even for that face that is within them, the face changed.

They suddenly discovered that instead of being within them, poisoning their inner peace, the face was outside them. As we praise God with all that is within us, whatever has no right to be within is expelled.

You cannot force yourself to stop thinking about the "face of your ill" but, when you begin to praise God even for that face, it loses its dominating power within and takes its proper place as part of your life experience. The psalmist prays to God: "Let your face shine upon your servant; save me in your steadfast love" (Psalm 31:16). "The face of God", shining within your heart, will banish the tormenting "face of your ills". While broken relationships are always painful and a source of sadness, they should never exercise a controlling and dominating power within us

A consoling image

In a wonderful image the psalm then tells us what God does for us: "[God] crowns us with steadfast love and mercy." When we come to God with our own sins and with the wounds inflicted on us by the sins of others, God never finds fault with us, never says it was all our own fault. Rather, he places on our head a beautiful crown of his love and compassion. At times we find it hard to receive this crown. We have become so accustomed to blame, blaming ourselves for our own misfortunes and being blamed by others for their misfortunes, that we often have to struggle with being unconditionally accepted and loved. Yet that is how God receives us, with total regard and delight. Even in our worst moments God assures us that we are the apple of his eye, that we are precious in his sight, that he loves us with an everlasting love. Our sins have never made us less precious to God. Despite all our sinful weaknesses we remain the image and likeness of God and as a sign of his abiding faithfulness God places on our head the crown of his compassion and love.

Take some time to work with this image. Try to visualise what a crown of compassion and love might look like. Identify some of the precious stones in that crown: amazing divine love, reassuring acceptance, unconditional forgiveness, the encouraging word. God wants to crown you with all of that.

Healing our image of God

God makes known to us why he relates to us in this forgiving way. Psalm 103 continues:

> The Lord is compassion and love,
> slow to anger and rich in mercy.
> His wrath will come to an end;
> he will not be angry for ever.
> He does not treat us according to our sins
> nor repay us according to our faults.

It is not just a question of God having compassion for us in our sinfulness. God reveals to us that in his very nature he is compassion and love. Being compassion, God can only relate compassionately; being love, God can only relate lovingly. So often, our greatest sin is not believing this. We tend to make God into our own image. We know that when people treat us badly we are sorely tempted to give them a bit of their own medicine. We expect God to be like us and deal with us in the way in which we so often deal with others. That is why God has to reveal to us that he is so different from us. God says, "let them return to the LORD, that he may have mercy on them, and to our God, for he will abundantly pardon. For my thoughts are not your thoughts, nor are your ways my ways, says the LORD. For as the heavens are higher than the earth, so are my ways higher than your ways and my thoughts than your thoughts" (Isaiah 55:7-9).

So often what we need healing most of all is our image of God. It is so easy to imagine that God must think and feel in the same way that we do ourselves. We can, therefore, form an image of God which makes it hard for us to be open and trusting in our approach to God in prayer. If I feel vindictive when I am hurt, I may be harbouring the fear that God feels vindictive when I sin against him or against my neighbour; if I have the urge at times to "get even" or "get my own back", I may unconsciously fear that God is the same. But God cannot be like that because God is "compassion and love". My thoughts are not his thoughts and my ways are not his ways. A missionary sister writes from Ecuador:

> Like many people of my generation – nearing sixty – I grew up with a stern father, and an image of God the Father as very strict – demanding perfection from me all the time, with that infamous "big book" ready to jot down my failures. Obviously I failed in my religious life. Nobody could live up to what I thought was expected of me. So I left, and tried to find happiness in possessions and addictions. God my Father waited patiently, lovingly and through many failures and mistakes, he drew me back to himself. During a retreat before coming out here the true image of God my loving Father was revealed to me and I'm still discovering the wonders of his goodness. I am now working in a slum area of Ecuador trying to help his poor children. I brought back a plaque from Kinnoull: "I will never forget you, I have carved you on the palm of my hands" and it hangs on my wall as a constant reminder. The one phrase I carried away from Kinnoull (thanks to Fr Charlie) is that I am precious in his eyes.[4]

When this sister's image of God was that of a stern father, demanding perfection at every turn, she didn't have the strength to live her life as a religious. When, however, the true image of God her loving Father was revealed to her she had the strength to work for the poor in a slum in Ecuador. She had sought happiness in possessions and addictions. Now she finds fulfilment in doing the Father's will in serving the poor.

It is good to take time to examine our image of God in this regard. As we reflect on our image of God we may quickly begin to detect where our image is simply the reflection of ourselves and has nothing at all to do with the revelation that God has given to us about his own inner nature.

Jesus is the full revelation of God. In what Jesus is and does we see what our God is and does. We see Jesus relating to everyone with respect, love and kindness; he forgives people's sins, he heals the sick, he sets people free from evil spirits, he is for ever encouraging and consoling people. He says to us, "If the Son makes you free, you will be free indeed" (John 8:36). Jesus has come to save us from our sins, to fill us with the Holy Spirit and to bless us with the gift of eternal life. That is how Jesus portrays God his Father to us, the God of mercy and compassion. And that is the image of God that we seek to hold in our hearts. An image that encapsulates mercy and compassion, love and generosity, tenderness and care, faithfulness and encouragement.

How God deals with our sins

The next verse of our psalm gives us a vivid, pictorial image of how God deals with our sins when we repent:

> For as the heavens are high above the earth
> so strong is his love for those who fear him.
> As far as the east is from the west
> so far does he remove our sins.

God places an infinite distance between our sins and ourselves, once we turn to God for forgiveness. It can be difficult to accept this. When you do something wrong, you are inundated with guilt and you might be feeling that you can never really get rid of it, that your sin, somehow, will always be around to remind you that you are no good. That is not God's way. As we turn to God for forgiveness our sins are wiped out. Totally removed from us. There is nothing God loves more than to say to us, "Your sins are forgiven." At his last supper with his disciples, when he instituted the Holy Eucharist, Jesus "took a cup, and after giving thanks he gave it to them, saying, 'Drink from it, all of you; for this is my blood of the covenant, which is poured out for many for the forgiveness of sins'" (Matthew 26:27-28). In his supreme manifestation of love, Jesus died for our sins. As he himself said, "No one has greater love than this, to lay down one's life for one's friends. You are my friends if you do what I command you. I do not call you servants any longer, because the servant does not know what the master is doing; but I have called you friends, because I have made known to you everything that I have heard from my Father" (John 15:13-15).

It is so healing to ponder the friendship that Jesus is offering to us. Even if you were to lose every other friend you ever had, you will not lose Jesus' friendship, so long as you remain close to him. Jesus delights in forgiving us our sins. But the one thing he asks us to do is to share his forgiveness with those who offend us. In fact, the nature of his forgiveness is such that if we do not share it with others we cannot hold on to it ourselves. He teaches us this truth by way of a compelling parable. When St Peter asked him how often we should forgive, "seven times?" Jesus replied, "Not seven times, but, I tell you, seventy-seven times" (Matthew 18:22). Then he told his disciples this parable:

> For this reason the kingdom of heaven may be compared to a king who wished to settle accounts with his slaves. When he began the reckoning, one who owed him ten thousand talents was brought to him; and, as he could not pay, his lord ordered him to be sold, together with his wife and children and all his possessions, and payment to be made. So the slave fell on his knees before him, saying, "Have patience with me, and I will pay you everything." And out of pity for him, the lord of that slave released him and forgave him the debt. But that same slave, as he went out, came upon one of his fellow slaves who owed him a hundred denarii; and seizing him by the throat, he said, "Pay what you owe." Then

his fellow slave fell down and pleaded with him, "Have patience with me, and I will pay you." But he refused; then he went and threw him into prison until he would pay the debt. When his fellow slaves saw what had happened, they were greatly distressed, and they went and reported to their lord all that had taken place. Then his lord summoned him and said to him, "You wicked slave! I forgave you all that debt because you pleaded with me. Should you not have had mercy on your fellow slave, as I had mercy on you?" And in anger his lord handed him over to be tortured until he would pay his entire debt. So my heavenly Father will also do to every one of you, if you do not forgive your brother or sister from your heart. (Matthew 18:23-35)

That parable of the unmerciful servant contains the whole Gospel teaching on forgiveness. "Forgive us as we forgive them." God takes us at our word. If we refuse to forgive, he cannot forgive us. If our refusal comes from a deep wound, God wants to heal that wound; if our refusal is the result of a hardened heart, God wants to give us the grace of conversion and a "new heart". Either way, God wants us to be forgiving, just as he is forgiving, because that is the only way in which we can hold on to God's forgiveness. The grace to forgive brings with it your greatest freedom, the healing of the hurts you have received. And most of all, by forgiving you become like God.

EXERCISE
- Centre yourself, using the techniques we learned in the first chapter of this book.

- Bring yourself to bodily stillness and calm.

- Reflect on one experience of God's forgiveness which you have had in your life.

- Become grateful to God for that forgiveness.

- Is there anybody in your life with whom you should be sharing that forgiveness right now?

- What grace do you need to share that forgiveness, the grace of inner healing or the grace of the new heart?

- Do you want to ask God for that grace?

- Now focus again on your breathing.

- And bring yourself gently back to the world.

Notes

1   *The Grail Psalms: A New Translation* (London: HarperCollins, 1963).

2   *Confessions of St Patrick* (New York: Doubleday, 1938), chapter 34.

3   St Bernard, *Sermon on the Song of Songs*, 61.

4   Correspondence to the authors.

About the Authors

Fr Jim McManus, a Redemptorist priest, is Rector of St Mary's Centre of Spirituality in Perth, Scotland. For the past thirty years he has been involved in spiritual renewal work through preaching retreats and missions, directing renewal courses and conducting workshops and seminars on the healing ministry. He is author of numerous books published by Redemptorist Publications, including *The Inside Job, The Healing Power of the Sacraments* and *Healing in the Spirit.*

Dr Stephanie Thornton C Psychol AFBPsS is a psychologist with thirty years' experience of studying the human mind and understanding, values, attitudes and emotions. She has published many books and articles. She is author of *Children Solving Problems,* published by Harvard University Press; and *Growing Minds: Introduction to Cognitive Development* and *Understanding Human Development,* both by Palgrave Macmillan. Now retired, she converted to Catholicism while head of the psychology department at Sussex University.